ACKNOWLEDGMENTS

The abridgments of *Interracial Housing: A Psychological Evaluation of a Social Experiment,* by Morton Deutsch and Mary Evans Collins (University of Minnesota Press, 1951); *The People's Choice: How the Voter Makes Up His Mind in a Presidential Campaign,* by Paul F. Lazarsfeld, Bernard Berelson, and Hazel Gaudet (Columbia University Press, 2nd Edition, 1948) and *Dynamics of Bureaucracy,* by Peter M. Blau (University of Chicago Press, 1955) are printed here with the permission of the publishers of the books. The abridgments have been read and approved by the authors. The selection from *Union Democracy: The Inside Politics of the International Typographical Union* (Free Press, 1956) by S. M. Lipset, Martin A. Trow and James S. Coleman, which appears here under the title "Union Democracy and Secondary Organization," is printed with the permission of the Free Press. "Biographies in Popular Magazines" by Leo Lowenthal, which appeared in *Radio Research 1942–43* (Bureau of Applied Social Research, 1944) edited by Paul F. Lazarsfeld and Frank Stanton, is printed here with the permission of Professor Lazarsfeld and the author.

Contents

AMERICAN SOCIAL PATTERNS

Introduction

A hundred years ago, when Auguste Comte coined the word *sociologie,* he conceived of this as the culmination of human knowledge. This noble if somewhat outdated vision has had a kind of perverse fulfillment; for sociology, though it has synthesized little, has indeed become marvelously eclectic. Partly because sociologists have no body of consistent theory from which to start, partly because they are not agreed on where they want to go, they have meandered off in all directions, and in their wanderings they have incorporated large sections of other social sciences. The amorphous character of sociology is indicated by the list of this volume's authors, who include among their number psychologists, social psychologists, and political scientists—and who might have included, with a different choice of essays, anthropologists, economists, geographers, or even philosophers.

This very heterogeneity, which developed principally out of flaws and lacks, has recently come to be recognized as also something of an advantage. Society is most fruitfully analyzed as a unit whenever its physical and functional elements are too closely interrelated to be clearly seen in isolation. For example, the economic or the military policy of a modern state cannot be understood by itself; but each of these marks the range of the problems that economics and political science, respectively, propose to handle. Similarly, neither the study of human nature apart from its cultural milieu nor the analysis of the market relations of "economic men" is now regarded as adequate, and the psychologists and economists breaking out of these traditional bounds often meet in such an expression of interdisciplinary cross-fertilization as this volume. The fact that sociology cuts across these arbitrary lines makes it the most confused, and perhaps most confusing, of all social sciences; but it is also the one that offers the most promise for the future.

What characterizes the rubric "sociology" today? What have the following five studies of American society in common? One of the essays—that by Deutsch and Collins on race relations—says something new on a topic as old as American sociology. The other four exemplify subject matters and methodological techniques that have been developed more recently—the Lazarsfeld-Berelson-Gaudet panel study of voting behavior, Lowenthal's content analysis, the Lipset-Trow-Coleman study of democracy in a trade union, and Blau's study of bureaucracy. That is to say, one criterion in selecting these works has been an attempt to reflect at least part of the wide range of problems with which American sociologists are currently concerned.

The unity among these essays consists not in their subject matter but in their frame of reference: the significant unit in society is not the individual but the group. Thus, in the liberal theory of democracy, the electorate is made up of a number of discrete indi-

viduals who have no joint will until they have expressed it through the mechanism of an election; while
in *The People's Choice* each voter makes up his mind
according to the pressures and cross-pressures of the
social groups he belongs to. Lipset and his coworkers
try to show that internal democracy in a trade union
results from such factors as the existence of a network
of clubs and informal social relations among the members. Lowenthal analyzes magazine articles not in
terms of their authors' psychology but in relation to
the social trend. The prejudices that each person has
are learned; and, as Deutsch and Collins show, what
he learns is set by the social framework of his life. In
Blau's study an attempt to increase the productivity of
an office staff by encouraging a competitive spirit is
shown to have been self-defeating, for productivity
depends in part on the group cohesion that this effort
broke down. In short, any study based on the premise
that society is something more than the sum of the
individuals who compose it is "sociological"; and this
frame of reference can be applied to any area whatever
of human life.

American sociology in particular has another unify-
ing characteristic underlying its diversity that tends
to set it off from its counterparts in other countries—
namely, its dominant concern with social research. Indeed, for the world at large, this *is* American sociology:
Gallup and Kinsey are household names almost as
much in Birmingham and Bombay as in Brooklyn.
Thus another feature of this volume is that it offers five
empirical studies, the accounts of ten persons who left
the academic cloister armed with significant questions,

grappled with the raw data they found, and brought these into some sort of temporary order. The pure theorists and the library researchers, however important their work, are not represented here. Nor are the most influential empirical studies represented—such works as the *Middletown* books, the *Yankee City* series, *The American Soldier*, *The Authoritarian Personality*, *Sexual Behavior in the Human Male* and *Female*, *Management and the Worker*. No abridgment of approximately forty pages could do justice to either the virtues or the flaws of these giants, which average about a thousand pages each.

The essay by Lowenthal was reprinted without change from the out-of-print publication in which it originally appeared. The Lipset-Trow-Coleman selection contains a part of a very large volume on the International Typographical Union. The other three selections are abridgments of books of about two hundred pages, reporting research that one man or a small team took a year or two to complete. The number of such middle-sized works is large and seems to be growing, and some of them offer perhaps the best introduction that an intelligent layman could find to sociology. Typically, they ask a question of which the significance is generally recognized and they seek to answer it with research methods that, however crude, are yet infinitely superior to the suppositions and prejudices of the untrained. Although a conscientious effort has been made to present the reader with the meat of these three studies, it must be emphasized that they all offer much more than could be included here. Thus for each abridgment the first title in the list of recommended additional readings ought to be the volume that was abridged.

Another general characteristic of the five studies is that they are written in the vernacular, with a minimum of that special language that sociologists have developed for easier communication among themselves. Lay readers tend to regard professional jargon, when it is not simply bad writing, as a ponderous effort to disguise a slight content by an elaborate form; and they are certainly often right in this judgment. However, jargon does have its legitimate functions. Sociologists write under a special difficulty, for they attempt to make objective statements about subjects on which most people hold rather firm opinions. One way of avoiding the bias that the usual words often connote is to coin an equivalent one. Thus, for example, the authors of *The People's Choice* discuss the relation between voting predilections and what is ordinarily termed "social class," but they prefer to use the somewhat barbarous phrase "socioeconomic status," for this is both more precise and less colored with feeling tones. On the other hand, jargon may be useful in emphasizing a point. When Deutsch and Collins write, for example, that "people tend to behave the way they are expected to behave," such a series of ordinary English words gives no hint that this assertion represents a radical revision of the notion still widely held among the general public that "human nature" is static. That is to say, if the reader finds a few unfamiliar or "obvious" words or phrases in the following pages, he should not immediately assume that they are there only because of the authors' ineptness.

A final general characteristic of these five studies is their relevance to sociological theory. In the nineteenth century sociologists built all-inclusive theoretical systems, all of which have since disintegrated. Today, in a reaction against such armchair theorizing, many American sociologists concentrate on gathering "the facts." But for any social phenomenon being studied, there is an infinity of "facts"; the ones that are perceived, are judged to be significant, depend on the theoretical framework of the observer. Good research follows from questions that theory has suggested, and it contributes to theory by giving tentative answers to those questions.

"The recent history of sociological theory," as Professor Robert K. Merton of Columbia University has noted, "can in large measure be written in terms of an alternation between two contrasting emphases"—between theorists pure and simple and radical empiricists. The first stress what is significant, apart from its truth; the second what can be validated, apart from whether it is significant. But "there is no logical basis for their being ranged *against* each other. Generalizations can be tempered, if not with mercy, at least with disciplined observation; close, detailed observations need not be rendered trivial by avoidance of their theoretical pertinence and implications."

In this sense these five empirical essays are also five modest contributions to sociological theory. Studies of this dimension are the bricks and mortar out of which a general theory of society will one day be built.

WILLIAM PETERSEN
Boulder, Colorado

Interracial Housing[*]

MORTON DEUTSCH & MARY EVANS COLLINS

The significance of race relations to a democratic society has long been recognized by social scientists. Yet, among literally thousands of books, monographs, and articles devoted to problems of race relations, there have been very few studies focused on changing prejudices. Most have been oriented toward the present or the past rather than toward the future; they have been concerned with finding out what exists and how it has come to exist rather than with uncovering techniques for social change. Most of those few studies in the reduction of prejudice, moreover, have been limited to the analysis of a single stimulus (such as a college course, a motion picture, a visit to a Negro hospital) which was probably of minor importance relative to other influences in the subject's social milieu. The often discouraging and inconclusive results of such investigations may well reflect the comparatively superficial nature of the influences being studied. The pervasive-

[*]The authors wish to acknowledge gratefully the financial support received from the Marshall Field Foundation, the suggestions and criticisms from their colleagues at the Research Center for Human Relations at New York University, and the work of Dorothy Barrett and Esther Rankin in collecting the data concerning the children in the projects.

ness of discrimination and prejudice suggests that the social and psychological barriers to democratic race relations are too strong to give way to any but strong counterinfluences.

The social scientist is rarely in the position to create these influences himself. He has neither the political power nor the financial resources to arrange a major social experiment. Nevertheless social "experiments" are going on all the time; or, more precisely, major attempts at producing social and psychological changes of one sort or another are commonplace. With the aid of scientific controls the social scientist can occasionally convert an attempt at social change into a social experiment. This was the purpose of our study. We wanted to investigate the effects upon prejudice of possibly one of the most important social "experiments" in the area of race relations—the establishment of public-supported, non-segregated interracial housing projects. Unfortunately, as in most such innovations, social scientists did not participate in the design of this one. The problem we faced was to convert, ex post facto, a social change into a scientific social experiment.

There are many reasons why residential segregation can be considered to be of central importance to intergroup relations in general. First of all, residential segregation brings with it, as a natural consequence, segregation in many other areas of living. Racially segregated neighborhoods tend to bring with them segregation in schools, recreational centers, shopping districts, playgrounds, theaters, hospitals, leisure-time facilities, etc. Thus one result of residential segregation is that prejudiced whites have little opportunity to see

Negroes in social contexts which bring out the fundamental *condition humaine* of Negroes and whites. They do not see the Negroes, for example, as school children disliking homework, as expectant mothers in their first pregnancy, as tenants complaining about their landlords, or as breadwinners facing a contracting labor market.

Residential segregation is important in yet another way. Next to employment discrimination segregation is probably the most significant way by which Negroes, as a group, are disadvantaged. In the North residential segregation of Negroes has always resulted in increased competition for a limited number of dwelling units, with the consequence that they have invariably paid higher rentals for poorer accommodations. With limited incomes high rentals have resulted in severe overcrowding and rapid physical deterioration of the houses. The economic and psychological burdens resulting from these conditions have contributed notably to a high incidence of delinquency, broken homes, emotional instability, and the general brutalization of life. These characteristics of Negro ghettos also tend to support the rationales for prejudice, helping to perpetuate the vicious circle which Gunnar Myrdal and others have fully documented.

Apart from run-down neighborhoods in a process of racial transition, the major instances of a break with the traditional practice of residential segregation in the United States have occurred in public housing. While the usual pattern, even in public housing, is complete segregation, with Negroes and whites living in separate housing projects, there are important exceptions. These exceptions and the variations among them provide, in effect, a natural social experiment that permits those engaged in carefully controlled social research to gather valuable information about the conditions which make for wholesome race relations.

The Research Problem: The Occupancy Pattern

To orient ourselves to the field of interracial housing, we interviewed forty-two housing officials throughout the country. Many studies were suggested by this survey: the effects of different policy decisions, the effects of different management procedures, the effects of different kinds of tenant activities. From our survey of housing officials and from our theoretical expectations we had reason to believe that the occupancy pattern, perhaps more than any other single factor, established the framework which serves to define the social meanings and the social limits of race relations. Hence, we chose to study the impact of different occupancy patterns: *the integrated interracial pattern* (families are assigned to apartments without consideration of race) and *the segregated biracial pattern* (Negro and white families live in the same project but are assigned to different buildings or to different parts of the project).

From the point of view of race relations what are the essential differences between an integrated project and such a segregated project? Theoretical considerations led us to believe that the two types differ mainly with respect to (1) the physical and functional proximity of Negro and white families, (2) the social norms regarding race relations implicit in this policy decision by an official public authority, and (3) the relation of the project to the broader community.

The predictions with regard to social relations across racial lines that we intended to test were based upon the following hypotheses: (1) the amount of contact between any two persons will increase as the distance between their places of residence decreases; and (2) as the amount of contact between any two persons increases, they will tend to like each other more. From these hypotheses we expected that (1) there will be more frequent and more intimate contacts between Negro and white families in an integrated than in a segregated project; and (2) a prejudiced white person who moves into an integrated project, if he stays long enough, is more likely to develop friendly feelings toward the Negroes in the project than if he were to move into a segregated project.

With regard to social norms we anticipated that (3) they would be more favorable to friendly relations between Negroes and whites in the integrated projects than in the segregated projects. There are several reasons for advancing this prediction. First of all, people tend to behave the way they are expected to behave: the expectations of others in a social situation, particularly if these others are important to the individual, help to define what is the appropriate behavior. There is little doubt that a public housing authority is significant in the lives of project residents, if only because it controls their only means of obtaining decent housing at a low rental. Furthermore, the policy of integration or segregation is an official decision implicitly carrying public sanction, and as such it helps to establish standards for what one "should" or "should not" do. The policy of segregation implies that Negroes and whites should be kept apart; the policy of integration implies that race should not be a criterion for distinguishing among tenants.

In addition to its direct psychological impact in shaping social norms the policy decision has indirect effects upon social norms through the physical environment that it creates for race relations. Interracial contact is affected by the physical nature of the occupancy pattern. The differences in interracial behavior resulting from the different occupancy patterns have consequences for the social norms which emerge in the projects. Thus, a housewife in the integrated projects is more likely to have friendly relations with Negroes and, in addition, is more likely to see other housewives having the same.

The fact that a housing project typically exists as a part of a larger community rather than in isolation means that the attitudes toward interracial relations of people outside the project affect those in the project. This is why discrepancies between the project and the community in interracial standards are likely to have special consequences for the tenant in an integrated project. We could, therefore, predict that (4) the salience of the interracial aspects of the project would be greater in the integrated than in the segregated project.

Much accumulated experience seems to indicate that an issue that is important to a number of people in common frequently draws these people closer together. The issue provides a source of conversation, a basis of common experience; it calls for increased socializing as a means of providing mutual support for opinions and as a way of working out solutions to the problems which the issue represents. Thus (5) the relations among the white residents would be more friendly in an integrated than in a segregated project. This is a rather surprising possibility which had not occurred to us when we began to plan our research.

Evidence is being gathered to indicate that frequent and intimate, socially sanctioned, equal-status contacts between Negroes and whites tend to reduce prejudice among whites. One could expect that (6) white tenants in an integrated project would come to have less prejudice toward Negroes than their counterparts in segregated projects.

To sum up, we have presented the essential differences between housing projects with segregated biracial and integrated interracial occupancy patterns. Calling upon existing sociopsychological knowledge and theory, we have attempted to predict the effects of these differences upon (1) social relations across racial lines, (2) the standards for behavior with respect to the other race, (3) the general pattern of social relations in the project, and (4) interracial attitudes.

The Research Procedure

In the abstract the research design called for by our hypothesis that proximity leads to friendliness was relatively uncomplicated. First of all, we carefully selected the segregated and integrated projects we were to study so that they were as equivalent as possible in all relevant respects other than the occupancy pattern. Second, we stretched our funds so as to study two projects of each type. And, third, we collected data about factors other than the occupancy pattern, to determine whether our results could be explained in terms of these other factors.

In 1949, New York was one of the few cities in the country with integrated interracial housing projects. At that time Newark had a segregated policy in its biracial public housing projects. These two cities are, of course, both large metropolises, with considerable similarity in their racial and ethnic composition. Their proximity and the similarity of their business and industry result in a constant interchange of residents. Newspapers from New York can be found on the newsstands of Newark; radio and television programs originating in either city reach the populations of both. That is to say, inhabitants of the two cities are subject to essentially similar cultural influences.

Once the cities were chosen, a number of different factors had to be kept in mind in selecting the projects to be included in our study: age of the project, racial ratio, type of neighborhood, ethnic composition of management, building structure, and project size. The preliminary survey had indicated that the racial ratio was considered to be a vital factor in influencing interracial relations, and we decided that our principal criterion for selecting "matched" projects in the two cities would be that of racial ratio. Finding that Newark-I had two Negroes to every white and New York-I had 70 per cent Negroes, we chose these two projects as our first matched pair. Newark-II divided 50-50 in its racial ratio; the Negro-white ratio for New

York-II was approximately 40-60. Since the composi-
tions of these last two projects were the most similar
of the remaining possible pairings, they were chosen
as the second pair.

Perhaps the greatest difference in the housing authorities of the two cities is in size. The housing program in New York demands an extremely complex
administrative setup, thereby removing the individual
tenant further from the central office than in Newark.
Both authorities adhere to the same over-all regulations
laid down by federal authority; both began their programs at approximately the same time. Both administrations include a person on the central office staff
whose major responsibility is handling individual tenant problems. The neighborhoods of the matched
projects were found to be strikingly similar. All four
had both Negro and white employees on the management staff.

We decided to collect our data primarily from white
housewives, randomly selected. The home is largely
the domain of the woman, who spends more time in it
than anyone else; she is, by and large, the initiator of
activities and contacts that develop directly out of the
home. Since it was not financially feasible to interview
Negro and white housewives in equal proportion, we
decided to interview more white housewives, as a
result of our conviction that prejudiced interracial attitudes are more crucial among whites than among
Negroes. All in all, we interviewed approximately 100
white and 25 Negro housewives in each of the four
projects. (Thus, in the balance of this report, all respondents are white except those specifically identified

as Negro.) In addition, 24 Negro and white adolescent boys and girls were interviewed in one project in each of the two cities.

The interviews, which took place in the respondent's apartment, lasted about an hour and a quarter; some ran over two hours. During the interview data were obtained in five major categories:

1. The attitudes of the housewives toward living in the project. Each housewife was asked what she liked most and least about the project; what her feelings were about public housing, the neighborhood, the apartment, etc.; the anticipations she had before moving into the project; her future plans; and her feeling in general toward people in the project.

2. Attitudes toward the other race. A series of questions attempted to uncover the attitudes of the housewife toward Negroes (or whites), her feelings about them, her "knowledge" and beliefs about them, and her feelings about living in the same project with them.

3. The amount and intimacy of contact with other women in the project. Questions were asked about neighborly contacts (such as visiting, shopping together, minding children, going to movies together), friendships, how one gets to know people, etc.

4. The social supports for attitudes. The housewife was asked, for example, to tell how her relatives, her friends, people in the project, the management staff, etc., would react to her being friendly with Negro (or white) people.

5. The characteristics of the housewife. A comprehensive list of questions was asked about the housewife —her age, number of children, her activities, her educa-

tion, her religion, her interests, etc.—to obtain information about the comparability of the populations in the projects we were studying.

Control of the Data

We endeavored to plan the study in such a way that the differences we are reporting could be explained only by the differences in the occupancy pattern—not, for example, by differences between the prior interracial experiences and attitudes of the tenants in the two types of projects. That is, it was necessary to consider the following questions from the outset: Did the attitudinal differences between the housewives in the integrated and the segregated projects exist prior to their residence in public housing and perhaps *cause* them to move into the one or the other type of project? Or did the differences in attitudes *result* from their living in the different types of projects? The evidence supports the second alternative:

1. As a result of the desperate need for housing among those eligible for low-income public housing, so few who could get housing refused it that there was little opportunity for selection on the basis of attitudes. The rate of refusals was low—estimated as less than 5 per cent (for all reasons, only a few of which are relevant to race) in both New York and Newark. Voluntary move-outs from the projects under study were also very infrequent.

2. If, however, the prejudices of some eligible people were sufficiently strong to make them resist the attraction of housing incomparably superior to that generally available to low-income groups, we should expect that

they would reject equally the integrated and the segregated biracial projects we studied. All four projects are located in predominantly Negro neighborhoods; a prejudiced person could not ignore the pervasive "Negro" impression visually created by the neighborhoods of all four projects.

3. To a certain extent the possibility of moving into an all-white project in Newark (most of the public housing projects in Newark were all-white) might have created more resistance in the prejudiced person to moving into a biracial project than was the case in New York, where there were only integrated projects. To the extent that this prevailed in Newark, however, it worked in a direction contrary to our findings; i.e., it had the effect of bringing less prejudiced tenants into the Newark projects that were studied.

The questions we asked to determine the housewife's previous experiences with Negroes, her education, her religion, and her political attitudes threw further light on the comparability of the people in the various projects. It is not unreasonable to assume that if the housewives moving into the New York projects were less prejudiced before their moving, this lesser degree of prejudice would be associated with their previous experiences with Negroes, the amount of their education, their type of political belief, their religion, or some combination of these factors.

The housewives in the two types of projects were not completely comparable on factors, other than the occupancy pattern, which conceivably might influence interracial contact and attitudes. Table 1 summarizes the major differences. There were more Jews in the

New York projects; and a large number of the Jewish housewives in New York-II, who had had little schooling in the United States, spoke mostly Yiddish. The difference in language between them and the Negro tenants acted as a barrier to intimate communication and contact. The people in the New York projects tended to be somewhat more liberal politically than in Newark. The women in New York-I had relatively more education than those in the other projects. In both New York projects, religion, education, and political attitudes were highly interrelated. Those with liberal political attitudes were most likely to be Jewish and relatively well educated, and those with most education were also most likely to be Jewish. This is not to assert the converse—that most of the Jews in the projects were liberal or relatively well educated. On the contrary, only a minority were politically liberal and only a small percentage had completed high school.

A priori it is extremely difficult to tell how important differences in religion, education, and political attitudes are in relation to prejudice. In any case, it is clear that in the analysis and presentation of our results it will be necessary to control these population differences in order to attribute causal significance to the occupancy pattern.

Getting to Know People of the Other Race

The prejudiced white person, because of his prejudice, does not get to know Negroes intimately in an equal-status relation. His prejudices combine with social custom to prevent him from having the types of experiences with Negroes which would destroy his

TABLE 1. Percentages of White Housewives

INTEGRATED PROJECTS

	New York-I (90)	*New York-II* (102)
Religion		
Protestant	18%	4%
Catholic	43	19
Jewish	32	74
Other	7	3
Education		
Only public school	30	47
Some high school	35	28
Completed high school or more	34	15
Attended school outside U.S.	1	10
Political attitudes		
Liberal	36	36
Middle-of-road	25	33
Conservative	39	31
Previous contact with Negroes		
(1) Has had Negro friends..	29	18
Has not had Negro friends	71	82
(2) Has worked with Negroes	36	26
Has not worked with Negroes	64	74
(3) Has lived on same block with Negroes	20	16
Has not lived on same block with Negroes	80	84

prejudices. Hence the main source of information about Negroes comes to be the "experiences," beliefs, and feelings of other prejudiced members of his own group. As a consequence, members of the prejudiced group, through contact with each other, tend mutually to confirm and support one another's prejudices. A vicious circle is established whereby, without personal with Designated Characteristics

	SEGREGATED PROJECTS	
	Newark-I (100)	*Newark-II* (101)
Religion		
Protestant	23%	16%
Catholic	67	40
Jewish	7	42
Other	3	2
Education		
Only public school	51	42
Some high school	33	36
Completed high school or more	14	14
Attended school outside U.S.	2	8
Political attitudes		
Liberal	18	26
Middle-of-road	37	36
Conservative	45	38
Previous contact with Negroes		
(1) Has had Negro friends..	30	19
Has not had Negro friends	70	81
(2) Has worked with Negroes	33	33
Has not worked with Negroes	67	67
(3) Has lived on same block with Negroes	22	33
Has not lived on same block with Negroes	78	67

The figures in parentheses indicate the number of cases on which the percentage figures are usually based. There are slight variations in the number of cases from table to table because of no responses, unclear answers, omitted questions, etc.

experience with members of a minority group, contact with the prevailing attitude toward them provides the "experience" to support a prejudice.

Perhaps the first problem that faces the person who

wishes to change the attitudes of a prejudiced individual is that of breaking through this vicious circle so as to bring to bear upon the bigoted the experiences necessary to a change in attitudes. Something must be done to "prevent" the prejudiced person from selectively avoiding the experiences which might disrupt his prejudices. The housing shortage has created an opportunity to establish such a situation. Very few of the white tenants in either the segregated or the integrated projects we have studied would have moved into a project containing Negro families if they had been guided solely by their attitudes. Their intense need for housing compelled them to move into a situation they would otherwise have avoided.

By our hypothesis the opportunities to get to know members of the other race should be greater in the integrated projects. Let us consult the data.

In the interview we asked the housewife to indicate whether she thought that a person who moved in would "be likely to get to know any colored people in the project." The differences between responses of the housewives in the two types of projects were striking. More than 95 per cent of the women in each of the two integrated projects asserted that a person would get to know some Negroes in the project. In contrast, in the segregated projects the large majority were quite convinced that no such likelihood existed. One housewife in Newark-I summed up a typical reaction quite aptly in her response: "We're in separate parts. They stay on their side and we stay on our side."

The interviews with the Negro housewives gave similar results. *All* of the Negro housewives in each of the integrated projects asserted that a Negro who moved in would "be likely to get to know some white people in the project"; in contrast, almost two thirds of the Negro housewives in the segregated projects said there was no such likelihood.

In the integrated projects the places of interracial contact most frequently mentioned were the apartment buildings themselves, through laundry facilities located in or near their buildings, or outside on benches. In contrast, the relatively small percentage of housewives in the segregated projects who indicated a likelihood of getting to know Negroes in the project specified as the most likely meeting place the stores outside the project where they did their shopping. Thus the segregated project provided only incidental occasions for interracial contact; the contacts that did take place occurred under rather casual circumstances and were of brief duration.

Physical proximity is not sufficient by itself to explain the above results. There was a sizable number of apartments in the segregated projects physically as close to Negro buildings as the adjacent buildings in the integrated projects. Clearly, other factors were also at work. Two of them may be (1) the social norms with respect to interracial associations in the project; (2) the tendency of friends and acquaintances to introduce each other to friends and acquaintances.

A deeply ingrained attitude such as prejudice, which constantly receives so many social reinforcements, will be changed only as a result of intensive experiences with which the prejudice cannot be reconciled. A superficial acquaintance with one's Negro neighbors may not be sufficiently intimate to provide such experiences. Little is known about the conditions that promote or hinder the development of close, friendly relations among neighbors in an apartment house or housing project. Thus, a priori, there is no particular reason to expect that Negro and white people living as next-door neighbors in a housing project are likely to get to know each other with sufficient intimacy to destroy stereotypes. Nevertheless, one would, of course, anticipate more intimacy of social relations between Negroes and whites in the integrated projects. From our interviews we can provide three measures of intimacy of social relations: (1) getting to know "pretty well"; (2) getting to know "best"; and (3) degree of "neighborly relationship."

In the integrated projects friendships and acquaintanceships with Negroes were not limited to Negroes living in the same building. Sixty per cent of the women in New York-I and 25 per cent of those in New York-II knew some Negroes from other buildings "pretty well"; in contrast, only 3 per cent of the women in the two segregated projects reported knowing any Negroes in the project "pretty well." "Know pretty well" is, of course, a subjective matter. We asked the following question: "Do you usually call the women you know pretty well here in the project by their first or last names?" We followed this with: "How many women do you know 'pretty well'?"

None of the housewives in the segregated projects included Negroes among the five persons each knew best in the project. In contrast, 62 per cent of the women in New York-I and 27 per cent of those in New

York-II indicated that at least one of the women they knew "best" was Negro. Similarly, only three of the 50 Negro housewives interviewed in the two segregated projects stated that at least one of the women they knew "best" was white; in the integrated projects more than half of the Negro women interviewed made this assertion.

Some of the crucial differences between the two types of projects, we have suggested, arise out of the fact that neighborly contacts are physically more possible in the integrated projects. Merely from living as next-door neighbors in one type of project and not in the other we would expect that the opportunities to engage in neighborly activities would be vastly different. We asked questions about the following types of activities: (1) visiting back and forth; (2) helping one another out, for example, with shopping or with taking care of the children, or with caring for the sick; (3) informal club activities, such as card clubs and sewing or ironing clubs; and (4) going out together, such as to the movies, shopping, or "downtown." We constructed a crude index of neighborly relations by counting the number of different types of activities engaged in. The differences were clear-cut. Only 1 per cent of the housewives in Newark-I and 4 per cent in Newark-II had any type of neighborly contact with Negro women; in contrast, the figures for New York-I and New York-II were 72 per cent and 39 per cent respectively. Similarly, 44 of the 50 Negro housewives in the segregated projects indicated *no* neighborly relations with white women; this was true for only 14

TABLE 2. Percentages of White Housewives with

| | INTEGRATED PROJECTS | |
	New York-I	New York-II
Political Attitudes		
Liberal	36% (31)	60% (35)
Middle-of-road	22 (23)	59 (32)
Conservative	26 (35)	61 (31)
Education		
Only public school	39 (26)	68 (47)
Some high school	30 (30)	50 (28)
Completed high school or had		
some college	16 (31)	53 (15)
Religion		
Protestant	31 (16)	25 (4)
Catholic	38 (39)	58 (19)
Jewish	13 (23)	67 (72)

of the 49 Negro women interviewed in the New York projects.

As has been noted, the respondents in the New York projects had somewhat different backgrounds from their counterparts in Newark. One may legitimately ask whether or not these variations provide an explanation for the differences in interracial contacts so far found to characterize the two types of projects.

As Table 2 shows, it seems to make little difference what type of person you are, or what kind of background you have, or what type of attitudes you possess; if you live in a segregated project, almost inevitably you will have no neighborly relations with the Negroes in the project. From other research we would expect that interracial contacts would occur more often among those politically more liberal. However, when we consider the "liberals" from the segregated projects and

No Neighborly Relations with Negroes in the Project

	SEGREGATED PROJECTS	
	Newark-I	*Newark-II*
Political Attitudes		
Liberal	100% (18)	92% (26)
Middle-of-road	100 (37)	95 (36)
Conservative	97 (45)	100 (38)
Education		
Only public school	100 (50)	93 (42)
Some high school	100 (33)	100 (34)
Completed high school or had		
some college	100 (14)	93 (14)
Religion		
Protestant	100 (23)	100 (16)
Catholic	98 (66)	98 (40)
Jewish	100 (7)	95 (41)

The figures in parentheses represent the number of individuals on which the percentages were computed. In some cases the numbers are so small as to make the percentages relatively meaningless; they are included only for consistency of presentation. The reader should interpret them accordingly.

the "conservatives" from the integrated projects, this expected finding is reversed. Whereas almost all of the "liberals" in the segregated projects (100 per cent of 18 and 92 per cent of 26—Table 2) were entirely devoid of neighborly relations with Negro tenants, this can be said of only a considerably smaller percentage of the "conservatives" in the integrated projects (26 per cent of 35 and 61 per cent of 31).

Space prevents us from presenting tables in which interracial contacts of housewives who are equated simultaneously with respect to education, religion, and political attitudes are compared. A typical example of what we find when making such comparisons will suffice. If politically conservative Catholic housewives with an elementary-school education only are contrasted for the two types of projects, we obtain the following results: *None* of the 28 such housewives in the two segregated projects engaged in neighborly activities with Negro women; in the integrated projects, however, 9 out of the 14 housewives with such characteristics had neighborly relations with Negro women.

Thus it is clear that the occupancy pattern markedly influences interracial contact. Moreover, its effects are strong enough to reverse the relation that prior research has often documented between prejudiced attitudes and such other factors as liberalism and conservatism.

Social Norms Created by the Occupancy Pattern

A housing project may be seen as composed of many informal groups organized around various types of goals. These groups are intricately connected through their overlapping memberships. Within this complex network it is likely that group standards or social norms will develop relevant to issues that are collectively important to the interconnected groups. We have suggested that, as a consequence of the public sanction of friendly interracial relations implicit in the integrated occupancy pattern, the social norms in the integrated projects will be more favorable to friendly interracial relations than those in the segregated projects.

In the interviews with the white housewives we asked two questions to elicit value statements about intimate associations with the Negroes in the project. The questions were: "Are there any reasons why you think it might be better for you to *have* (*not* to have) much to do with the colored families in the project?" A considerably higher percentage of the white women in the segregated projects (55 per cent and 36 per cent) gave "reasons" why it might be better *not* to have much to do with the colored families in the project than did those in the integrated projects (20 per cent and 12 per cent). Considerably more people in the segregated projects (49 as contrasted with 11 in the integrated projects) developed or retained an ideology that "It's best for colored and white not to mix" or "We should stay on our side and they should stay on their side" or "It's best not to have anything to do with them." Housewives in the segregated projects frequently mentioned spontaneously the social pressure from other whites not to associate with Negroes: "They'd think you're crazy if you had a colored woman visit you in your home. They'd stare at you and there'd be a lot of talk." Another said, "I used to be good friends with a colored woman who worked with me at Westinghouse before I moved here. She lives in the other side of the project but I never have her over to my apartment—it just isn't done. Occasionally I go over and visit her."

No instances of social pressure not to mix with Negroes were mentioned in the integrated projects. A woman in New York-I responded, "You should be neighborly with the people next door. If you get into trouble, they'll help you out and if they need something you should help them out." A young mother in

New York-I said, "They resent you if you're not friendly. You're liable to find yourself in plenty of trouble around here if you try to be snooty." That is, the housewife in the integrated project was more likely to be exposed to direct social pressure to be friendly.

Of all the informal sanctions employed to make member behavior conform to the social norms of the group, gossip and public notoriety are perhaps the most important. To avoid group hostility and to avoid being the objects of malicious gossip, people learn to anticipate how others will react if they behave in certain ways. These anticipations serve to guide the individual so that he conforms with the norms of the group. We asked the housewives to indicate the reactions they anticipated from their husbands, from their friends in the project, and from the management staff if they were friendly with Negro families. Those in the integrated projects anticipated more favorable reactions in all three categories than those in the segregated projects, who typically expected disapproval from their husbands and friends in the project. In both types of projects the management staff was seen as being more approving than disapproving. Having an interracial staff, one can assume, tended to counter the effects on the tenants' perception of management policy, which the occupancy pattern might be expected to create.

The Negro housewives in all the projects anticipated relatively more favorable than unfavorable reactions to interracial association from their husbands, friends within the project, and management staff. However, the number anticipating favorable responses was con-

sistently greater in the integrated projects. These findings are as one would expect. The social norm for
Negroes with respect to racial relations is generally to
favor friendly interracial associations; they want to
break down rather than maintain segregation. However, in the segregated projects, partly as a defense
against the insult of segregation, countersentiments developed to a certain extent: "If they don't want to be
friendly, we don't want to be friendly either."

The guide for behavior to the person living in an
integrated project is that of friendly interracial association; the standard implicit in the segregated pattern
is that of avoidance, with the connotation that interracial association brings trouble or that it is socially
degrading.

Social Norms and Social Relations within the Project
No project exists in complete isolation. It exists in
a community and the attitudes in the community toward interracial relations have effects on the people in
the project. This is why several questions in the interview were aimed at the reactions of relatives and
friends outside the projects to friendly interracial contacts.

In all of the projects considerably more housewives
anticipated that their friends in the broader community
would disapprove, rather than approve, of their being
friendly with the Negro tenants. However, in both New
York projects, a percentage somewhat higher than in
the other projects reported having friends who would
approve. While we have no systematic evidence on the
point, one possible explanation of this finding might

be that the housewives in the New York projects more frequently rejected and were rejected by former friends who disapproved of their association with Negroes. Thus one housewife said, "I have lost a lot of my old friends who wouldn't want to visit me because I am neighborly with some of the Negro people here. But I've also made a lot of new ones." Another woman exclaimed, "They wouldn't be my friends for long if I knew they were prejudiced." However, one cannot select one's relatives. All of the housewives in the four projects who mentioned relatives said that the latter would disapprove of their being friendly with Negroes.

For the housewife in the segregated project the reaction of the broader community presents no problem, since she has little contact with Negroes and the standard implicit in the policy of separating Negro and white families does not suggest such contact. In contrast, the housewife in an integrated project experiences a dilemma in this respect. As one of them said: "I'm very friendly with the [Negro] lady next door; we're in and out of each other's place all the time. That's it. A problem comes up when my relatives, especially my mother-in-law, visit. They don't like the idea of me living next door to Negroes. You know my friend sometimes just pops in. Well, I don't want to hurt my friend—I got to get along with my mother-in-law—it's a problem all right."

As a result of these cross-pressures, the housewife in the integrated project was more aware of the interracial aspects of the project than her counterpart in the segregated project. Whether her attitude toward it was positive or negative, the interracial composition of the project was more prominent in her thinking. During the course of the interview (before the interviewer asked any questions specifically related to Negroes) the housewives in the integrated projects spontaneously mentioned the Negro group or the interracial aspects of the project both earlier and more frequently than those in the segregated projects.

We have suggested that an issue that is of concern to a number of people in common frequently draws these people closer together. Their mutual concern provides a common bond of experience, a basis of intimate conversation. It results in increased socialization in the course of working out solutions to the problems the issue represents, and gives those concerned an opportunity to find support for their opinions. It is only natural, since no conventional, well-established customs exist for the handling of these problematic social situations (certainly none of the standard books of social etiquette provides ready answers), that these women share their experiences in searching for a satisfactory solution.

As has been indicated, there were considerably more neighborly activities (visiting with one another, helping one another, going out together, and informal or club activities) among the women in the integrated than in the segregated projects. Since these activities involved fairly close and intimate relations, they may be taken as a crude measure of the social cohesion of the project. Table 3 presents another indication of cohesion, namely, the number of close friends the respondents had in the project. It is clear that, by and

TABLE 3. Percentage of White Housewives Indicating

	INTEGRATED	PROJECTS
Number of Close Friends	*New York-I* (85)	*New York-II* (86)
None	18%	26%
1–4	37	39
5 or more	45	35

large, the women in New York had more close friends in their projects than those in Newark.

When asked to describe what the people in their project are like, the housewives in the integrated projects drew a much more favorable picture of their co-tenants, white as well as Negro, than did their counterparts in the segregated projects. In New York-I 70 per cent, and in New York-II 60 per cent, used such phrases as: "They're very nice," "Everyone has a friendly 'Hello,'" "People are very neighborly here." In contrast, only about a third of the women in the segregated projects had positive remarks to make about each other.

It seems likely that the greater friendliness that characterized the relations of housewives in the integrated projects resulted in some measure from the cross-pressures to which they were exposed. Partly as a defense and partly as a means of solidifying themselves in the face of outside disapproval, the housewives were drawn closer together, with the resulting social gain of increased project cohesion. A complementary loss of some friends outside the project might be expected, but actually this did not occur. It was true that housewives in the integrated projects reported losing some former friends who were prejudiced, but they also a Specific Number of Close Friends within the Project

	SEGREGATED PROJECTS	
Number of Close Friends	Newark-I (94)	Newark-II (94)
None	34%	32%
1–4	44	42
5 or more	22	26

Some housewives did not indicate a specific number of close friends; these responses are not included. The figures in parentheses indicate the number of cases on which the percentage figures were computed.

reported gaining new friends. The results indicated no difference between the housewives in the two types of projects in number of close friends outside the projects.

To sum up, the social norms of the integrated projects with respect to race relations diverged more from the norms of the broader community than did those of the segregated projects. As a consequence of this divergency, the housewife found herself exposed to various cross-pressures that made the issue of interracial relations an area of fairly prominent interest and concern. The integrated projects were characterized by a friendlier, more cohesive social atmosphere. The white housewives in the integrated projects knew each other better, liked each other better, and did more things together; in other words, not only did they have closer relations with Negroes, but also with the other white people in their project. There was no evidence to indicate that this gain in social cohesion of the integrated project resulted in or from an over-all loss of friendships with people outside the project. On the

Table 4. Percentages of White Housewives Who Ascribed

Attributes Most Frequently Mentioned	INTEGRATED PROJECTS	
	New York-I (90)	New York-II (102)

Positive Attributes

Helpful, do you favors, good neighbors	28%	18%
Polite, respectable	14	20
Sociable, friendly, cheerful	33	15
Try to improve themselves	17	3
They're people, human beings	17	36
No positive attributes mentioned	17	27

Negative Attributes

Low-class, noisy, rowdy, impulsive, primitive, drink a lot	9	14
Inadequate parental control; children are destructive	18	13
"Inferiority complex" about prejudice	19	12
Troublemakers, aggressive, dangerous	10	13
No negative attributes mentioned	68	61

other hand, there was some evidence to indicate that the housewife in the segregated project, by shunning activities in which Negro tenants might participate, lost opportunities for friendly social relations with members of her own race as well.

Attitudes toward Negroes

Relations between Negro and white housewives in the integrated projects were preponderantly friendly, while in the segregated projects most housewives did not have any relations with the Negroes in the project.

Designated Attributes to Negroes in the Project

Attributes Most Frequently Mentioned	SEGREGATED PROJECTS	
	Newark-I (100)	Newark-II (101)
	Positive Attributes	
Helpful, do you favors, good neighbors	1%	0%
Polite, respectable	11	7
Sociable, friendly, cheerful	6	11
Try to improve themselves	3	3
They're people, human beings	19	27
No positive attributes mentioned	54	52
	Negative Attributes	
Low-class, noisy, rowdy, impulsive, primitive, drink a lot	33	25
Inadequate parental control; children are destructive	17	23
"Inferiority complex" about prejudice	1	2
Troublemakers, aggressive, dangerous	36	31
No negative attributes mentioned	46	53

Percentages may add up to more than 100 per cent because some housewives mentioned more than one attribute. The figures in parentheses indicate the number of cases on which the percentage figures were computed.

Similarly, more than half of the Negro housewives in each of the integrated projects reported friendly relations with the white women in the project; on the other hand, somewhat over 80 per cent in each of the segregated projects reported no social relations with white women.

Table 4 summarizes the positive and negative attributes ascribed to the Negroes in the project. It is apparent that more housewives in the integrated projects than in the segregated projects ascribed positive attributes to the Negro people, while the reverse is true for negative attributes. It is interesting to note that, of those who included any positive attributes, relatively more in the integrated projects mentioned attributes (such as helpfulness) that are related to neighborliness. Other attributes mentioned frequently were politeness, respectability, sociability, friendliness, and cheerfulness. The negative attributes cited by housewives in the segregated projects were, for the most part, the usual stereotypes; Negroes are "impulsive," "primitive," "troublemakers," "dangerous," etc. In the integrated projects one of the most frequently mentioned negative attributes was "inferiority complex" about prejudice. Someone commented, "They have it in for whites. They've been beaten down and hurt for so long that they're out for their revenge." It would seem likely that this attribution of "sensitivity" or "inferiority complex" to Negroes implies more of an appreciation of the Negro as a person than the more usual negative attributes. It recognizes in him understandable psychological characteristics and a human motivation that, although having troublesome consequences, allow for the possibility of empathy.

One would anticipate that the stereotypes or the conceptions the housewife had of the Negro were likely to change more readily than the feelings underlying them. Thus of the housewives in all four projects a higher proportion held the Negro tenants in high esteem than desired to be friendly with them. The differences between the housewives in the two types of projects were somewhat greater with respect to "friendly feelings" than to "esteem." One interpretation of this result would support the notion that "feelings" are more basic than "beliefs," that beliefs are a more superficial layer of the personality than feelings, so that a change in beliefs is a necessary but not always sufficient condition for a change in feelings. In other words, even the superficial contacts between Negroes and whites in the segregated projects might be enough to destroy the belief of many housewives that Negroes are basically inferior, whereas more intimate experiences would be necessary to produce friendly feelings.

It has been frequently observed that attitude changes of this type may have little generality. Thus Marie Jahoda has written:

The organizer of an interracial camp who has watched members of different groups drawing closer and judging each other on an individual basis rather than in terms of group membership, sometimes is shocked to find that some of the participants return to their communities and continue a pattern of strictly segregated life. Trade union officials in Detroit who had consistently advocated and implemented a policy of nonsegregation and educated their membership to the acceptance of this principle were disturbed to learn that some of their staunchest union members had actively participated in the race riots in 1943. . . . Changes produced in one situation have little effect on behavior in another context.

Nevertheless, according to the judgments of the interviewers, the housewives in the integrated projects, as compared with those in the segregated projects, had become more favorably disposed toward the Negro people in general, as well as toward the Negroes in their projects. These changes in attitude, however, were not as extensive; that is, not all the housewives who changed their attitudes as a result of experiences with some Negroes generalized their changes to include other Negroes. Perceiving Negroes as equals provides only the opportunity for the development of friendly feelings; for this opportunity to be fully realized intimate social contacts with Negroes on an equal-status basis seem to be necessary also.

During the course of the interview the housewives were asked to state whether they agreed with, were not sure about, or disagreed with the following statements: "Generally speaking, colored people are lazy and ignorant." "In general, colored people can't be trusted." And, "There's something different and strange about colored people; it's hard to tell what they're thinking and planning, or what makes them tick." The purpose of these questions was to provide us with additional information about the nature and frequency of the stereotypes of Negroes held by the housewife. Presenting the stereotypes in the affirmative, rather than in the negative, made it less likely that the housewife would disagree. In everyday life people encounter these stereotypes as we phrased them, and it seemed more instructive to get some notion of how the housewives would react when confronted with the statements in this form.

In the two New York projects 50 per cent and 67 per cent disagreed with at least two of these stereotypes; in the Newark projects this was true of 33 per cent of the tenants in one and 42 per cent in the other. These differences may be taken as further evidence that the attitudes of many housewives in the integrated projects have changed, not only toward the Negroes in the project, but also toward the Negro people in general. However, the difference between the two types of projects was less than with other attitudes tested. The most commonly accepted stereotype in all projects was the third. This unrationalized statement of difference seems to represent a last stronghold for prejudiced beliefs retreating before conflicting experience.

Perhaps the most striking data come from the reports of the housewives themselves about their own attitude changes toward Negroes in general. We asked the housewives a series of questions like the following: "Can you remember what you thought colored people were like before you moved into the project?" "How much have your ideas about colored people changed since you have lived in the project?" If some change, "In what ways have they changed?" and "What do you think made you change your ideas?" Responses to such questions must always be evaluated with caution because of the distorting effects of recall. We have examined the data for differential distortion between the two types of projects but could find no such indications of this.

The majority of housewives in the integrated projects reported that their attitudes had become more favorable, only a few less favorable. In the segregated projects there was also some increase in the number favorable, though these were offset to a greater extent

TABLE 5. Percentages of White Housewives Reporting

	INTEGRATED PROJECTS	
Present Attitude	*New York-I*	*New York-II*

Originally Unfavorable

	(31)	(58)
Favorable	55%	50%
Less unfavorable, but not favorable	29	24
Still unfavorable (no change) .	10	23
Even more unfavorable	6	3

Originally Neutral, Indifferent, or Ambivalent

	(26)	(26)
Favorable	69%	50%
Still neutral (no change)	23	46
Unfavorable	8	4

Originally Favorable

	(32)	(15)
Even more favorable	34%	13%
Still favorable (no change) ...	60	87
Less favorable	6	0
Unfavorable	0	0

by those who had become less favorable. The *net gain* (percentage of housewives reporting favorable changes minus the percentage reporting unfavorable changes) was 56 per cent and 55 per cent for the integrated projects; for the segregated it was 5 per cent and 20 per cent.

As shown in Table 5, no matter what her original attitudes were, if a housewife changed them as a result of her experiences in an integrated project, she would be most likely to change them in a more favorable

Designated Present and Past Attitudes toward Negroes

	SEGREGATED PROJECTS	
Present Attitude	*Newark-I*	*Newark-II*
Originally Unfavorable		
	(39)	(36)
Favorable	8%	8%
Less unfavorable, but not favorable	28	22
Still unfavorable (no change) .	54	59
Even more unfavorable	10	11
Originally Neutral, Indifferent, or Ambivalent		
	(47)	(47)
Favorable	24%	13%
Still neutral (no change)	70	76
Unfavorable	6	11
Originally Favorable		
	(13)	(17)
Even more favorable	15%	6%
Still favorable (no change) ...	85	70
Less favorable	0	6
Unfavorable	0	18

The figures in parentheses indicate the number of cases on which the percentage figures were computed.

direction. Relatively, she was most likely to change, however, if her original attitudes were unfavorable and least likely to change (as would be expected) if her original attitudes were favorable. In the segregated projects, if the housewife's original attitudes were unfavorable or neutral, any attitude change was also more likely than not to be reported in a favorable direction. This cannot be asserted unequivocally for those in the latter type of project who were originally favorably disposed toward Negroes.

Why did some housewives change and others not? Are there any clearly identifiable characteristics that make one housewife more likely to change attitudes than another? We offer our tentative suggestions without any statistical elaborations because the usual number of cases on which they are based is very small.

1. The people who reported no change had relatively fewer intimate contacts with Negroes. Proportionately fewer of them indicated a Negro as one of the persons they knew best in the project; considerably more of them stated that they had no neighborly activities in common with Negro women; comparatively fewer had had, prior to moving into the project, equal-status contact experiences with Negroes.

2. The people who reported change were relatively more cohesive members of the project community than those who did not. They liked the people in the project relatively more; they knew more people in the project, and were more likely to belong to an organization within the project, and were more likely to engage in neighborly activities with other women in the project.

3. The people who reported change were more likely to report that their friends expected them to be friendly with Negroes.

4. The people who reported no change were more likely to have low morale. They were more likely to dislike living in the project and to indicate distress or unhappiness in answer to the question: "Generally speaking, how happy are you with your present state of affairs?"

5. There seemed to be no clear-cut relation between reported change and political attitudes or religion (except that those who indicated regular religious observance were less likely to report change than those less regular in observance). However, younger housewives, housewives who identified themselves as "working class" rather than "middle class," and those who had had at least a high school education were more likely to report change.

6. And, as one would expect if our data are at all self-consistent, the housewives who reported change were less prejudiced and favored interracial housing more.

Which comes first? Was it the predisposition to change that resulted in more contact with Negroes, or was it the contact that caused the change? Did low morale make it less likely that a person would be friendly with his Negro neighbors, or did having Negro neighbors make for low morale? We cannot provide any conclusive answer to these questions with the data available from a study of this type.

In summary, considerable generalized changes in attitudes toward Negroes occurred among the people living in the integrated projects. It is clear, on the other hand, that not all housewives who came to respect and like their Negro neighbors extended their feelings to the Negro people in general. According to the responses of the housewives, approximately 60 per cent of the white women in the integrated projects became less prejudiced and only about 5 per cent more prejudiced. In contrast, about 75 per cent of the white women in the segregated projects indicated no reduction in prejudice; and of these approximately 10 per cent reported becoming more prejudiced.

Children in the Two Project Types

Perhaps the most impressive evidence of the effects of the occupancy pattern in guiding behavior came from the interviews with children. Twenty-four children in New York-I and the same number in Newark-I were interviewed. All were between the ages of 11 and 14. Half in each project were white, half Negro; half were girls, half boys.

Twenty of the 24 children interviewed in New York-I shared spontaneous activities, such as baseball, fishing, movies, and games, with members of the other race. In Newark-I only two Negro children (a boy and a girl) engaged in such activities with white children, and in both cases the white children were outside the project. These differences appear to be even more significant when one takes into consideration the fact that all of the Negro and white children in Newark-I attended unsegregated schools and that some of the children from the different sections of the project went to the same school. As a result of their contacts in school, all of the children had at least speaking acquaintances with members of the other race. Yet when they came home to the project, they shared no activities.

As one boy put it: "We play together at school and then return to our own side of the housing project and never see each other here." A twelve-year-old girl stated that she had made friends with a Negro girl at camp and she thought the girl was very nice. Both girls lived in the Newark project, but they never saw each other.

In unsegregated New York-I all but 2 of the 24 children interviewed visited in the homes of both their Negro and white friends in the project. Newark-I provided a sharp contrast: *none* of the 24 children interviewed visited in the homes of members of the other race in the project. One white child, however, visited in the homes of Negro friends *outside* the project. He explained this by saying, "Nobody visits in the houses on the other side of the project."

The interviews with the children made it appear that the white parents played a role in reinforcing this ideology. Thus one boy said, "My mother doesn't like Negroes and won't let me go around with them. She punishes me if I play with them." A white girl said her mother did not want her to visit Negroes, but she did not know the reason. In contrast, all but two of the children interviewed in New York-I said the Negro and white adults got along well together. Typically, when asked to express their parents' attitudes, they replied, "They see no differences between Negroes and whites."

The interviews with the children indicated how they themselves felt about living in their respective projects. Fifteen of the 24 children questioned in New York-I expressed enthusiasm for living in the project, describing it as "nice" or "fine," or saying, "It's fun to live here"; 6 described it as "okay" or "all right"; 3 indicated that they did not like it, of whom 2 stated they did not like to live among colored people. One of these 2 had been living there only four months and had no friends, white or Negro; the other indicated that her parents felt the same way.

In contrast, in Newark-I 20 of the 24 children were unenthusiastic about living there. Most of the white children among the 20 complained that they used to have a large playground on their side of the project that had been taken away from them. They expressed considerable feeling about this because the Negro children still had their playground on their side. Some expressed resentment because they were not permitted to form a club on the project unless the Negro children were allowed to join. The Negro children, while for the most part not directly criticizing the occupancy pattern, also were unenthusiastic about living in the project. They too expressed a sense of rivalry with the white children for the facilities and for the manager's approval.

Thus, while many other factors were undoubtedly also operating, it seems probable that the segregation of races (with the resulting competition for facilities) made the children in Newark relatively less enthusiastic about their project than the unsegregated children in New York. The children in New York-I, moreover, were considerably more favorable toward their project than their mothers. Many of the white mothers, with aspirations for their children oriented toward the future, were apprehensive about their children's close relations with Negro children (though they did not necessarily disapprove or discourage it); their children, as yet unconcerned with the prejudices of the broader community, enjoyed the community in which they lived.

Each housewife was asked to imagine that she was being questioned about the project by a friend who knew nothing about it, and was then asked, among others, the following question: "You know I have two children. . . . My girl is fourteen and my boy is nine. What would it mean for them to live in a project where there are colored and white families?" The views of the women in the two types of projects were somewhat different. A sizable minority of the housewives in the segregated projects (32 per cent in Newark-I and 15 per cent in Newark-II) said, "The colored kids and the white kids don't have much to do with each other. White kids stay on their side, colored kids on their side." None of the women in the integrated projects made such statements. Of those who asserted definite opinions, pro or con, about the effects of the racial composition of the project upon the children, in each of the integrated projects 56 per cent made positive statements, compared with slightly smaller proportions in the segregated projects.

Relatively more housewives in the integrated projects pointed out (in the words of a mother in New York-I): "This has been a wonderful experience for my children. They have had an opportunity to learn to be unprejudiced."

The negative evaluation of the women in Newark was most commonly expressed as a feeling that "children should be brought up with their own kind." In the integrated projects, however, the most common negative reaction was rather to the neighborhood and to the schools. Thus one New York housewife said, "The schools around here are awful. They're 90 per cent colored. There aren't enough teachers. I don't think they keep up the schools in colored sections too well. The good teachers won't come here. I want to move to ——, where I can send my boy to a better school."

It is interesting to note that, though we included in our questions about children a reference to a fourteen-year-old girl so as to stimulate responses indicating anxieties or problems in relation to the adolescent girl in a racially mixed project, we obtained relatively few answers that would indicate that intermarriage, as such, was a source of concern. Only 1 per cent of the women in each of the two segregated projects, 5 per cent in New York-II, and 12 per cent in New York-I indicated that white girls have specific problems. These women, for the most part, indicated that the white girls are socially handicapped by the fact that there were not so many white adolescent boys as there might be in an all-white neighborhood.

Summary and Conclusions

The integrated interracial projects in comparison with the segregated biracial projects were characterized by:

1. Many more instances of friendly, neighborly contacts between members of the different races.

2. A social atmosphere more favorable to friendly interracial associations.

3. A more closely knit project community.

4. More favorable attitudes toward Negroes in the project and also toward the Negro people in general.

5. More favorable attitudes toward living in an interracial project.

These behavioral and attitudinal differences between the tenants in the New York and Newark projects seem to result directly from the following differences between the two types of occupancy patterns:

1. The physical and functional proximity of Negro and white families is considerably greater in the integrated than in the segregated projects.

2. The social norms with respect to racial relations implicit in the official policy of a public authority are more favorable to friendly interracial relations in the integrated projects than in the segregated.

3. In a broader social milieu characterized by racial prejudice, the discrepancy between the social norms of the project and those of the broader community is greater for the residents in the integrated projects; it seems likely that this greater discrepancy has drawn the tenants in these projects closer together.

In an ex post facto study such as the present one change is always inferred rather than directly observed. From the existence of the marked differences in racial attitudes and behavior between the tenants in the integrated projects and those in the segregated projects, we *infer* that a considerable number of tenants in the former have become less prejudiced. This inference is supported by the reports of the housewives about their own attitude changes: there were many more women in the integrated projects who reported favorable attitude changes than there were in the segregated projects. The findings of related research, which indicate that equal-status contacts with Negroes are likely to reduce prejudices, also lend credibility to our inference. However, without an examination of alternative interpretations of the differences found between the two types of projects, we cannot be reasonably confident of the correctness of our interpretation.

We have reviewed the evidence we could bring to bear upon the question of the comparability of the interracial experiences and attitudes of the tenants prior to their moving into the two types of projects. All of the evidence—the psychological situation of the low-income family with a dire need for housing, the low rate of refusals by applicants, and the low rate of voluntary move-outs by tenants of the various projects we have studied, the reports of the housewives about their attitudes and experiences prior to moving into the projects, and our comparison of housewives in the two types of projects who are similar in education, religion, and political attitudes—all this evidence indicated that it is unlikely that the behavioral and attitudinal differences our data have revealed can be "explained away" in terms of an initial lack of comparability of the tenants in the two types of projects. Nor are the differences we found, so far as it is possible to tell, attributable to any idiosyncrasies in the projects we studied: tenant morale is high in all projects, no "special" efforts have been made to produce changes in attitudes in any of the projects, the projects in the two cities are similar in many respects (in ratio of Negroes to whites, in neighborhoods, in eligibility requirements, in age, in possessing interracial staffs, etc.).

Thus factors other than the occupancy pattern that might explain our results have been systematically examined and have been found to be inconsistent with the available data. It seems not unreasonable to conclude that, from the point of view of reducing prejudice and of creating harmonious democratic intergroup relations, the net gain resulting from the integrated projects is considerable; from the same point of view the gain created by the segregated projects is slight.

In examining the implications of our results we shall ask first about their meaning for interracial housing and then about their significance for intergroup relations in general. In what circumstances should we expect our results to hold for other comparisons of integrated and segregated projects? Under what conditions could we recommend the adoption of integrated housing in anticipation of results similar to those we found? From our results what can we conclude about factors affecting intergroup relations outside of public housing?

As a first step in considering the meaning of our results for interracial housing in general, let us examine the probability that our results would be confirmed in other comparisons of the two types of occupancy pattern. A study by Merton, West, and Jahoda of (in our terminology) a segregated biracial project in Pittsburgh reports results very similar to the ones we found for the biracial projects we studied in Newark. Our survey of housing officials experienced in interracial housing also supports the impression that the segregated project does not afford enough opportunities for intimate interracial contact to produce major attitude changes.

While we have studied integrated projects only in

New York, our interviews with housing officials in different parts of the country certainly suggest that New York is not the only place in which an integrated policy is possible. In such various cities as Hartford, Los Angeles, Philadelphia, and Seattle integrated interracial projects exist and they are managed without special difficulties. Though the population of New York City (and of the projects we have studied) is undoubtedly more polyglot and possibly more tolerant than in other sections of the country, the residential segregation of Negroes (apart from public housing) has been more rigid than in many other cities. Integration thus, in a sense, represents in New York a greater break with community practices than would be true for many cities. Moreover the integrated projects we studied in New York are far from ideal choices to demonstrate the feasibility of integrated housing. Many housing officials believe that when a project contains a population as high as 40 per cent Negro (both of the projects we studied had at least this proportion), it becomes more difficult for the white tenants to adjust to living in an integrated project. Both projects are also located in predominantly Negro neighborhoods, neighborhoods that are, in addition, rather deteriorated and characterized by considerable delinquency.

Further, although the tenant composition of the New York projects may differ from that to be expected in many other cities, it should be stressed that no matter what segment of the housewives we studied is considered, similar results were obtained with respect to changes in race relations and attitudes. That is, Catholic, Protestant, and Jew, the politically liberal and the politically conservative, and the well educated and the poorly educated adjusted to living in an integrated project and became less prejudiced despite initial forebodings.

While we see no reason for believing that integration is workable only in New York, the favorable results we found might not be expected under the following types of circumstances: where an "integrated" project contains only a token representation of Negroes, or, in other words, a proportion too small to result in any considerable amount of interracial contact; where attitudes in the community are extremely hostile, perhaps violently opposed to integrated housing—so much so that it becomes impossible to live in the project without bearing the brunt of the active opposition of the community; where the housing authority and project management do not firmly support and execute a policy of integration without equivocation—where, in other words, integration can be subverted by "complaints," by manipulation of management, etc.; where the members of the management staff are prejudiced; or where extremely inefficient management results in low tenant morale, with bickering and hostility characterizing the relations among tenants of all groups.

In the light of these judgments about the conditions under which our findings might be expected to hold, what can we recommend concerning the use of integrated housing in other cities? We are, in effect, rejecting the notion that has characterized much of sociological thinking in the field of race relations: the notion, originating with William G. Sumner, that "stateways cannot change folkways." The evidence of our study is that official policy, executed without equivocation, can result in large changes in beliefs and feelings despite initial resistance to the policy. Thus it is clear from our data that, although most of the white housewives in the integrated projects we studied did not, upon moving into the projects, like the idea of living in the same buildings with Negro families (and certainly the community as a whole did not favor it), a considerable change in attitudes and "folkways" has taken place as a consequence of their experiences resulting from a "stateway."

We believe (though additional research is obviously necessary to replace beliefs by verified knowledge) that the sociopolitical considerations throughout most of the North and in the West are such as to make integrated housing feasible; and in terms of democratic values, if it is feasible, it is preferable by far to the segregated pattern. The free mixing of Negroes and whites in buses and trolleys, in downtown cinemas, in shopping centers, and, to some extent, in schools and at work, the lack of legal or moral pressures to segregate, and the growing political significance of the Negro vote—all suggest its feasibility in much of the North and West. In contrast, the pervasive "Jim Crow" of the South, the legal and extralegal supports for prejudice and discrimination, the Negroes' almost complete lack of political rights and of political power, and the organized and semi-legalized violence to keep Negroes in an inferior status suggest that considerable political-economic change (internally or externally imposed) will be necessary before integration will be either a likely or a feasible policy in much of the South. In a sense we are on considerably firmer ground when we discuss the theoretical implications of our research. Other related studies made in rather different social settings in which more or less similar socio-psychological conditions were at work—in the Army, in industry, in the merchant marine, in universities, and in government agencies—all provide results in essential agreement with those of the present study. They all indicate that under certain types of conditions equal-status contacts with Negroes will result in a considerable change in the behavior and attitudes of the prejudiced person.

A POSTSCRIPT
by Louis Danzig, executive director,
Housing Authority of the City of Newark

A new policy for locating tenants is now in effect in Newark's eight public housing projects and will also apply to the three skyscraper developments soon to be constructed. That policy, one long favored by many of us, provides that henceforth all apartments are to be allocated on a basis of need, regardless of race, religion, and color. As a result, the partial segregation that has characterized public housing in Newark will no longer obtain. Instead of Negroes and whites being kept in separate buildings they are being assigned to apartments in the same buildings without regard to their race.

In large measure this change in fundamental policy

reflects the impact of the study reported here. The study has served as a catalyst to the re-examination of our basic interracial policies in housing and as a stimulus to their change. Many of us have long felt that the artificial separation of Negro and white families was an unwholesome procedure. However, until the study of Dr. Deutsch and Mrs. Collins we had no scientific evidence to substantiate our feelings. In supplying us with an objective picture of race relations in our projects, a picture that is faithful to our own impressions, their study dramatically focused our attention and that of the community at large on matters which, under the press of other business, we had tended to ignore.

The study did more than help to focus attention on the basic question of segregation in housing. Perhaps its most important consequence was its usefulness to those community groups concerned with intergroup relations and civil rights, such as the Essex County Intergroup Council. To such groups the study was an invaluable tool in creating the atmosphere that made it possible for the housing authority to adopt and execute a policy of non-segregation. I don't know how many meetings of such groups I attended, but invariably the Deutsch-Collins study was referred to and quoted. All these meetings were necessary and helpful. Without active support from community groups and the new state law prohibiting discrimination in public housing it would have been extremely difficult for us to adopt a change in policy.

A word about the change. Naturally, as we undertook the process of integrating our projects, we were beset by some anxieties. If, however, our Newark experience may serve as a guide, the change-over to a policy of non-segregation is not so difficult and troublesome as one anticipates. Some of our tenants (these are by far in the minority) have complained to us vociferously, but there has been no disruption of our projects. When the complainants met a firm, calm response from housing management, they invariably subsided. Our experience leads me to believe that if a housing authority, its executive director, and his staff show complete sincerity in the change and never retreat from their announced position with respect to non-segregation, the change will be successful. This, in any case, is what we have found to be true in Newark.

Even in this short time we have already observed significant changes in attitudes, as a consequence of which we shall undoubtedly find that as we break down the physical barriers between Negroes and whites in our projects, many of the social barriers will also disappear. We have been pleasantly surprised to find that some of the white tenants who were loudest in their objections to living next to Negro families have come to accept as *neighbors* the Negro families living next to them.

LOUIS DANZIG
November 1950

Suggestions for Further Reading

F. TREDWELL SMITH. *An Experiment in Modifying Attitudes toward the Negro* (New York: Teachers College, Columbia University, 1943). "The first scientific attempt to measure the effects on attitudes toward the Negro produced by cultural contacts with outstanding Negro individuals and groups in their own community."

BARBARA K. MACKENZIE. "The Importance of Contact in Determining Attitudes toward Negroes," *Journal of Abnormal and Social Psychology*, 43:4 (October 1948), 417–41. According to a study in three industrial plants, "acquaintance with Negroes of relatively high occupational status is an important factor in determining favorable attitudes of white persons toward Negroes."

[ARNOLD ROSE]. "Opinions about Negro Infantry Platoons in White Companies of Seven Divisions," Guy E. Swanson, Theodore M. Newcomb, and Eugene L. Hartley, *Readings in Social Psychology* (Society for the Psychological Study of Social Issues; New York: Holt, 1952), pp. 502–6. A summary of a War Department report showing that the more contact white infantrymen had had with Negro soldiers, the less prejudice was evidenced.

IRA N. BROPHY. "The Luxury of Anti-Negro Prejudice," *Public Opinion Quarterly*, 9:4 (Winter 1945–46), 456–66. On differences in prejudice among white merchant seamen according to differences in equal–status contact with Negroes.

GUNNAR MYRDAL et al. *An American Dilemma: The Negro Problem and Modern Democracy* (New York: Harper, 1944). A classic work on its subject. Chapter 16 deals with housing, Chapters 30 and 45 with the interaction between attitudes and social trends.

ROBERT K. MERTON *et al. Patterns of Social Life: Explorations in the Sociology and Social Psychology of Housing* (forthcoming).

DANIEL M. WILNER, ROSABELLE PRICE WALKLEY, and STUART W. COOK. *Human Relations in Interracial Housing* (Minneapolis: University of Minnesota Press, 1955). Another study of the racial attitudes of people living in public housing projects.

CHARLES ABRAMS. *Forbidden Neighbors* (New York: Harper, 1955). A detailed discussion of the problem, especially interesting for its description of the role of the federal government in encouraging and enforcing segregation in public housing.

Biographies in Popular Magazines*

LEO LOWENTHAL

RISE OF BIOGRAPHY AS A POPULAR
LITERARY TYPE

The following study is concerned with the content analysis of biographies, a literary type which has inundated the book market for the last three decades, and has for some time been a regular feature of popular magazines. Surprisingly enough, not very much attention has been paid to this phenomenon, none whatever to biographies appearing in magazines, and little to those published in book form.[1]

*This essay was written some fifteen years ago, during World War II. The subjects of the biographies, as transient as any popular fashion, have often passed into oblivion or quaintness; but the general points that the author makes from his analysis of these specific data remain as provocative today as when he wrote them.—EDITOR.

[1]Cf. Edward H. O'Neill, *A History of American Biography,* University of Pennsylvania Press, 1935. His remarks on p. 179 ff. on the period since 1919 as the "most prolific one in American history for biographical writing" are quoted by Helen McGill Hughes, *News and the Human Interest Story,* University of Chicago Press, 1940, p. 285 f. The book by William S. Gray and Ruth Munroe, *The Reading Interests and Habits of Adults,* Macmillan, New York, 1930, which analyzes readers' figures for books and magazines, does not even introduce the category of

It started before World War I, but the main on-rush came shortly afterward. The popular biography was one of the most conspicuous newcomers in the realm of print since the introduction of the short story. The circulation of books by Emil Ludwig,[2] André Maurois, Lytton Strachey, Stefan Zweig, etc., reached a figure in the millions, and with each new publication the number of languages into which they were translated grew. Even if it were only a passing literary fad, one would still have to explain why this fashion has had such longevity and is more and more becoming a regular feature in the most diversified publications.

Who's Who, once known as the title of a specialized dictionary for editors and advertisers, has nowadays become the outspoken or implied question in innumerable popular contexts. The interest in individuals has become a kind of mass gossip. The majority of weeklies and monthlies, and many dailies too, publish at least one life story or a fragment of one in each issue; theater programs present abridged biographies of all the

---

biographies in its tables on the contents of magazines, and applies it only once for books in a sample analysis of readers in Hyde Park, Chicago. The only comment the authors have to offer is: "There is some tendency to prefer biographies and poetry, especially in moderate doses to other types of reading except fiction" (p. 154). Finally, I want to quote as a witness in this case of scientific negligence, Donald A. Stouffer, *The Art of Biography in Eighteenth Century England*, Princeton University Press, 1941, who in his excellent and very thorough study says: "Biography as a branch of literature has been too long neglected" (p. 3).

[2] Up to the spring of 1939, 3.1 million copies of his books were sold: 1.2 million in Germany, 1.1 million in the U.S., 0.8 million elsewhere. (Cf. Emil Ludwig, *Traduction des Œuvres*, Moscia, 1939, p. 2.)

actors; the more sophisticated periodicals, such as *The New Republic* or *Harper's,* offer short accounts of the main intellectual achievements of their contributors; and a glance into the popular corners of the book trade, including drugstore counters, will invariably fall on biographies. All this forces the conclusion that there must be a social need seeking gratification by this type of literature.

One way to find out would be to study the readers' reactions, to explore by means of various interviewing techniques what they were looking for, what they think about the biographical jungle. But it seems to be rather premature to collect and to evaluate such solicited responses until more is known about the content structure itself.

As an experiment in content analysis, a year's publication of *The Saturday Evening Post* (*SEP*) and of *Collier's* for the period from April 1940 to March 1941 was covered.[3] It is regrettable that a complete investigation could not be made for more recent material, but samples taken at random from magazines under investigation showed that no basic change in the selection or content structure occurred in the few months following this country's entry into the war.[4]

[3]It should not be inferred that the results as presented here are without much change applicable to all other magazines which present general and diversified topics. From a few selections taken from less widely circulated and more expensive magazines, ranging from *The New Yorker* to *Fortune,* it seems very likely that the biographies presented there differ in their average content structure and therefore in their social and psychological implications from these lower-priced popular periodicals. The difference in contents corresponds to a difference in readership.

[4]Cf. footnote 12 of this article.

TABLE 1. Distribution of Biographies According to
for Selected Years

	1901–14 (5 sample yrs.)		1922–30 (6 sample yrs.)	
	No.	%	No.	%
Political life	81	46	112	28
Business and professional	49	28	72	18
Entertainment	47	26	211	54
Total	177	100	395	100
Yearly average of biographies..	36		66	

BIOGRAPHERS' IDOLS

Before entering into a discussion of our material we
shall look briefly into the fate of the biographical feature during the past decades.

Production—Yesterday

Biographical sections have not always been a standing feature in these periodicals. If we turn back the
pages we find distinct differences in the number of
articles as well as in the selection of people treated.

Table 1 gives a survey of the professional distribution of the "heroes" in biographies between 1901 and
1941.[5] It indicates clearly a tremendous increase in
biographies as time goes on. The average figure of
biographies in 1941 is almost four times as high as at
the beginning of the century. The biography has nowadays become a regular weekly feature. Just to illustrate how relatively small the number of biographies
was forty years ago: in fifty-two issues of the *SEP*
of 1901–02 we find altogether twenty-one biographies

[5]For the collection of data prior to 1940 the writer is indebted
to Miss Miriam Wexner.

Professions in *The Saturday Evening Post* and *Collier's*
between 1901 and 1941

	1930–34 (4 years)		1940–41 (1 year)	
	No.	%	No.	%
Political life	95	31	31	25
Business and professional	42	14	25	20
Entertainment	169	55	69	55
Total	306	100	125	100
Yearly average of biographies ..	77		125	

as compared with not less than fifty-seven in 1940–41.
The smallness of the earlier figure in comparison to that
of the present day is emphasized by the fact that non-
fictional contributions at that time far outnumbered the
fictional material. A fair average of distribution in the
past would be about three fictional and eight non-
fictional contributions; today we never find more than
twice as many non-fictional as fictional contributions
and in the majority of cases even fewer.

We put the subjects of the biographies in three
groups: the spheres of political life, of business and
professions, and of entertainment (the latter in the
broadest sense of the word). Looking at our table, we
find for the time before World War I very high interest
in political figures and an almost equal distribution of
business and professional men on the one hand, and
of entertainers on the other. This picture changes completely after the war. The figures from political life
have been cut by 40 per cent; the business and professional men have lost 30 per cent of their personnel,
while the entertainers have more than doubled. This
numerical relation seems to be rather constant from

1922 up to the present day. If we reformulate our professional distribution by leaving out the figures from political life, we see even more clearly the considerable decrease of people from the serious and important professions and a corresponding increase of entertainers. The social impact of this change comes to the fore strikingly if we analyze the composition of the entertainers. This can be seen from Table 2.

TABLE 2. Percentage of Biographies of Entertainers from the Realm of Serious Arts[a] in *The Saturday Evening Post* and *Collier's* for Selected Years between 1901 and 1941

(IN PER CENT OF TOTAL BIOGRAPHIES OF ENTERTAINERS IN EACH PERIOD)

Period	Percentage of entertainers from serious arts	Total no. entertainers
1901–14 (5 sample yrs.)	77%	47
1922–30 (6 sample yrs.)	38	211
1930–34 (4 yrs.)	29	169
1940–41 (1 yr.)	9	69

[a]This group includes literature, fine arts, music, dance, theater.

While at the beginning of the century three quarters of the entertainers were serious artists and writers, we find that this class of people is reduced by half twenty years later and tends to disappear almost completely at present.

As an instance of the selection of biographies typical of the first decade of the century, it is notable that out of the twenty-one biographies of the *SEP* in 1901–02 eleven came from the political sphere, seven from the business and professions, and three from entertainment and sport. The people in the political group are numerically prominent until before Election Day in the various years: candidates for high office, i.e., the President or senators; the Secretary of the Treasury; an eminent state governor. In the business world we are introduced to J. P. Morgan, the banker; his partner, George W. Perkins; James J. Hill, the railroad president. In the professions we find one of the pioneers in aviation; the inventor of the torpedo; a famous Negro educator; an immigrant scientist. Among the entertainers there is an opera singer, Emma Calvé; a poet, Eugene Field; a popular fiction writer, F. Marion Crawford.

If we look at such a selection of people, we find that it represents a fair cross-section of socially important occupations. Still, in 1922 the picture is more similar to that of the professional distribution quoted above than to the one which is characteristic of the present-day magazines. If we take, for example, *Collier's* of 1922, we find in a total of twenty biographies only two entertainers, but eight business and professional men and ten politicians. Leaving out the latter ones, we find among others: Clarence C. Little, the progressive president of the University of Maine; Leonard P. Ayres, the very outspoken vice-president of the Cleveland Trust Company; director-general of the United States Railroad Administration, James C. Davis; president of the New York Central Railroad, A. H. Smith; and the city planner, John Nolen. From the entertainment field we have a short résumé of the stage comedian, Joe Cook (incidentally, by Franklin P. Adams), and an autobiographical sketch by Charlie Chaplin.

We might say that a large proportion of the heroes in both samples are idols of production, that they stem from the productive life, from industry, business, and natural sciences. There is not a single hero from the world of sports and the few artists and entertainers either do not belong to the sphere of cheap or mass entertainment or represent a serious attitude toward their art as in the case of Chaplin.[6] The first quarter of the century cherishes biography in terms of an open-minded liberal society that really wants to know something about its own leading figures on the decisive social, commercial, and cultural fronts. Even in the late twenties, when jazz composers and the sports people are admitted to the inner circle of biographical heroes, their biographies are written almost exclusively to supplement the reader's knowledge of the technical requirements and accomplishments of their respective fields.[7] These people, then, are treated as an embellish-

[6]We have omitted from our discussion and our figures a number of very short biographical features which amounted to little more than anecdotes. These were published fairly regularly by the *SEP* until the late twenties under the headings "Unknown Captains of Industry," "Wall Street Men," sometimes called "Bulls and Bears," "Who's Who and Why," "Workingman's Wife," "Literary Folk."

[7]See, for instance, the *SEP*, September 19, 1925, where the auto racer, Barney Oldfield, tells a reporter details of his racing experiences and of the mechanics of racing and automobiles; September 26, 1925, in which the vaudeville actress, Elsie Janis, comments on her imitation acts and also gives details of her techniques. The same holds true for the biography of the band leader, Sousa, in the *SEP*, October 31, 1925, and of the radio announcer, Graham McNamee, May 1, 1926; after a few remarks about his own life and career, McNamee goes on to discuss the technical aspects of radio and his experiences in radio with famous people.

ment of the national scene, not yet as something that in itself represents a special phenomenon that demands almost undivided attention.

We should like to quote from two stories that seem to be characteristic of this past epoch. In a sketch of Theodore Roosevelt the following comment is made in connection with the assassination of McKinley: "We, who give such chances of success to all that it is possible for a young man to go as a laborer into the steel business and before he has reached his mature prime become, through his own industry and talent, the president of a vast steel association—we, who make this possible as no country has ever made it possible, have been stabbed in the back by anarchy."[8]

This unbroken confidence in the opportunities open to every individual serves as the leitmotiv of the biographies. To a very great extent they are to be looked upon as examples of success that can be imitated. These life stories are really intended to be educational models. They are written—at least ideologically —for someone who the next day may try to emulate the man whom he has just envied.

A biography seems to be the means by which an average person is able to reconcile his interest in the important trends of history and in the personal lives of other people. In the past, and especially before World War I, the popular biography lived in an optimistic atmosphere where understanding of historical processes and interest in successful people seemed to integrate pleasantly into one harmonious endeavor: "We know now that the men of trade and commerce

[8]*Saturday Evening Post*, October 12, 1901.

and finance are the real builders of freedom, science, and art—and we watch them and study them accordingly. . . . Of course, Mr. Perkins is a 'self-made man.' Who that has ever made a career was not?"[9] This may be taken as a classical formulation for a period of "rugged individualism" in which there is neither the time nor the desire to stimulate a closer interest in the organizers and organization of leisure time, but that is characterized by eagerness and confidence that the social ladder may be scaled on a mass basis.[10]

[9]*Saturday Evening Post,* June 28, 1902.

[10]Here and there we find a casual remark on the function of biographies as models for individual imitation. Cf., for instance, Mandel Sherman, "Book Selection and Self Therapy," in *The Practice of Book Selection,* edited by Louis R. Wilson, University of Chicago Press, 1939, p. 172. "In 1890 a book appeared entitled *Acres of Diamonds,* by Russell H. Conwell. This book dealt especially with the problems of attaining success in life. The author attempted to encourage the reader by giving examples of the struggles and triumphs of noted successful men and women. This pattern of encouraging the reader by citing examples of great men has continued, and in recent years a number of books have appeared in which most of the content dealt with case histories of noted individuals. Some psychologists have suggested that interest in autobiographies and biographies has arisen in part from the attempts of the readers to compare their own lives with those about whom they read, and thus to seek encouragement from the evidence of the struggles of successful people."

Helen M. Hughes in her suggestive study has not avoided the tendency to settle the problem of biographies by rather simplified psychological formulae. By quoting generously O'Neill, Bernarr MacFadden, and André Maurois she points to the differences of the more commemorative and eulogistic elements in earlier biographies and the "anxious groping for certainty of people who live in times of rapid change," which is supposed to be connected with the present interest in biography (see especially p. 285).

Consumption—Today

When we turn to our present-day sample, we face an assortment of people that is both qualitatively and quantitatively removed from the standards of the past.

Only two decades ago people from the realm of entertainment played a very negligible role in the biographical material. They form now, numerically, the first group. While we have not found a single figure from the world of sports in our earlier samples given above, we find them now close to the top of favorite selections. The proportion of people from political life and from business and professions, both representing the "serious side," has declined from 74 to 45 per cent of the total.

Let us examine the group of people representing non-political aspects of life. Sixty-nine are from the world of entertainment and sport; 25 from that which we called before the "serious side." Almost half of the 25 belong to some kind of communications profession: there are ten newspapermen and radio commentators. Of the remaining 15 business and professional people there are a pair of munitions traders, Athanasiades (118)[11] and Juan March (134); Dr. Brinkley (3), a quack doctor; and Mr. Angas (20), judged by many as a dubious financial expert; Pittsburgh Phil (23), a horse-race gambler in the "grand style"; Mrs. D'Arcy Grant (25), a woman sailor, and Jo Carstairs (54), the owner of an island resort; the Varian brothers (52),

[11]The figures in parentheses refer to the bibliography of stories studied, Appendix. Figures 1 to 57 refer to the *SEP* and 101 to 168 to *Collier's*. On the difference between the *SEP* and *Collier's*, see Appendix, Tables 4 and 5.

inventors of gadgets, and Mr. Taylor (167), an inventor of foolproof sports devices; Howard Johnson (37), a roadside restaurant genius; Jinx Falkenburg (137), at that time a professional model; and finally, Dr. Peabody (29), a retired rector of a swank society prep school.

The "serious" people are not so serious after all. In fact there are only nine who might be looked upon as rather important or characteristic figures of the industrial, commercial, or professional activities, and six of these are newspapermen or radio commentators.

We called the heroes of the past "idols of production": we feel entitled to call the present-day magazine heroes "idols of consumption." Indeed, almost every one of them is, directly or indirectly, related to the sphere of leisure time: either he does not belong to vocations that serve society's basic needs (e.g., the heroes of the world of entertainment and sport), or he amounts, more or less, to a caricature of a socially productive agent. If we add to the group of the 69 people from the entertainment and sports world the ten newspaper- and radiomen, the professional model, the inventor of sports devices, the quack doctor, the horse-race gambler, the inventors of gadgets, the owner of the island resort, and the restaurant-chain owner, we see 87 of all 94 non-political heroes directly active in the consumers' world.

Of the eight figures who cannot exactly be classified as connected with consumption, not more than three—namely, the automobile producer, Sloan; the engineer and industrialist, Stout; and the air-line czar, Smith—are important or characteristic functionaries in the world of production. The two armament magnates, the female freight-boat skipper, the prep-school head, and the doubtful market prophet remind us of the standardized protagonists in mystery novels and related fiction merchandise: people with a more or less normal and typical personal and vocational background who would bore us to death if we did not discover that behind the "average" front lurks a "human interest" situation.

By substituting such a classification according to spheres of activity for the cruder one according to professions, we are now prepared to present the vocational stratifications of our heroes in a new form. It is shown in Table 3 for the *SEP* and *Collier's* of 1940–41.

TABLE 3. The Heroes and Their Spheres

	Number of stories	Per cent
Sphere of production	3	2
Sphere of consumption	91	73
Entertainers and sports figures	69	55
Newspaper and radio figures	10	8
Agents of consumers' goods	5	4
Topics of light fiction	7	6
Sphere of politics	31	25
Total	125	100

If a student in some very distant future should use popular magazines of 1941 as a source of information as to what figures the American public looked to in the first stages of the greatest crisis since the birth of the Union, he would come to a grotesque result. While the industrial and professional endeavors were geared to a maximum of speed and efficiency, the idols of the

masses were not, as they were in the past, the leading
names in the battle of production, but the headliners
of the movies, the ball parks, and the night clubs. While
we found that around 1900 and even around 1920 the
vocational distribution of magazine heroes was a rather
accurate reflection of the nation's living trends, we observe that in 1941 the hero selection corresponded to
needs quite different from those of genuine information. They seemed to lead to a dream world of the
masses who no longer were capable or willing to conceive of biographies primarily as a means of orientation
and education. They received information, not about
the agents and methods of social production, but about
the agents and methods of social and individual consumption. During the leisure in which they read they
read almost exclusively about people who are directly,
or indirectly, providing for the reader's leisure time.
The vocational setup of the dramatis personae is organized as if the social production process were either
completely exterminated or tacitly understood, and
needed no further interpretation. Instead, the leisure-
time period seems to be the new social riddle on which
extensive reading and studying has to be done.[12]

[12]It will be very important to check later how far the war
confirmed, changed, or even reversed the trend. A few casual
observations may be mentioned.

The *New York Times* "Magazine" on July 12, 1942, published
an article "Wallace Warns Against 'New Isolationism.'" The
Vice-President of the United States is photographed playing tennis. The caption for the picture reads "Mr. Wallace's Serve."
This picture and its caption are a very revealing symbol. The
word "serve" does not refer to social usefulness, but to a feature
in the Vice-President's private life.

This remark can be supplemented by quoting a few issues of

Biographies in Popular Magazines

The human incorporation of all the social agencies taking care of society as a unity of consumers represents a literary type that is turned out as a standardized article, marketed by a tremendous business, and consumed by another mass institution, the nation's maga-

---

the *SEP* and *Collier's*, picked at random from their publications during the summer of 1942. While everywhere else in this study we have limited ourselves to the analysis of strictly biographical contributions, we should like, by quoting some of the topics of the entire issues we have chosen for this year, to emphasize the over-all importance of the spheres of consumption. Not only did the selection of heroes for biographies not change after America's active participation in the war, but many other of the non-fictional articles are also still concerned with consumers' interests.

Of the ten non-fictional articles in the *SEP*, August 8, 1942, five are connected with the consumers' world: a serial on Hollywood agents; a report on a hometown circus; a report on roadside restaurants; an analysis of women as book readers; and an essay on the horse and buggy. In an issue one week later, August 15, 1942, there is a report on the International Correspondence School; the continuation of the serial on the Hollywood agents; and a biography of the radio idol, Kate Smith. Or let us look at *Collier's*, which as a whole devoted a much higher percentage of articles to war topics than the *SEP*. Out of nine articles in the issue of July 4, 1942, five belong to the consumers' world. There is again one on the horse and buggy, another one on a baseball hero, a third one on an army comedian, a fourth one on a Broadway producer, and finally one on budget buffets. Three weeks later, on July 25, out of ten articles again five belong to the same category.

In other words, out of thirty-seven articles found in four issues of two leading popular magazines during the war crisis, not less than seventeen treated the gustatory and entertainment features of the average citizen.

There appears to be some cause for concern in the fact that so much of the fare presented to the reading public during the times immediately preceding the war and during the war itself was almost completely divorced from important social issues.

zine-reading public. Thus biography lives as a mass element among the other elements of mass literature.

Our discovery of a common professional physiognomy in all of these portraits encouraged us to guess that what is true of the selection of people will also be true of the selection of what is said about these people. This hypothesis has been quite justified, as we propose to demonstrate in the following pages. Our content analysis not only revealed impressive regularities in the occurrence, omission, and treatment of certain topics, but also showed that these regularities may be interpreted in terms of the very same category of consumption that was the key to the selection of the biographical subjects. Consumption is a thread running through every aspect of these stories. The characteristics we have observed in the literary style of the author, in his presentation of personal relations, of professions and personalities can all be integrated around the concept of the consumer.

For classification of the stories' contents we decided on a fourfold scheme. First, there are what one might call the sociological aspects of the man: his relations to other people, the pattern of his daily life, his relation to the world in which he lives. Second, his psychology: what the nature of his development has been and the structure of his personality. Third, his history: what his encounter with the world has been like—the object world, which he has mastered or failed to master. Fourth, the evaluation of these data the author more or less consciously conveys by his choice of language. Granted that this scheme is somewhat arbitrary, we think that our division of subject matter has resulted in a fairly efficient work sheet, especially when we consider the backward state of content analysis of this type.

As we studied our stories,[13] we looked almost in vain for such vital subjects as the man's relations to politics or to social problems in general. Our category of sociology reduces itself to the *private lives* of the heroes. Similarly, our category of psychology was found to contain mainly a static image of a human being to whom a number of things happen, culminating in a success that seems to be none of his doing. This whole section becomes merged with our category of history, which is primarily concerned with success data too, and then takes on the character of a catalogue of *"just facts."* When we survey the material on how authors evaluate their subjects, what stands out most clearly is the biographers' preoccupation with justifying their hero by means of undiscriminating *superlatives* while still interpreting him in terms that bring him as close as possible to the level of the average man.

PRIVATE LIVES

The reader may have noticed in public conveyances a poster called "Private Lives," depicting the peculiarities of more or less famous people in the world of science, sports, business, and politics. The title of this

[13]We proceeded to collect all the passages in the 125 stories pertaining to our four categories. It is not intended here to analyze the 2400 quotations exhaustively, but merely to present in the following chapters a few observations or hypotheses that their study suggested to us and that we hope may be stimulating to further research in content analysis.

feature is a fitting symbol for all our biographies. It would be an overstatement, but not too far from the truth, to say that these stories are exclusively reports on the heroes' private lives. While it once was rather contemptible to give much room to the private affairs and habits of public figures, this topic is now the focus of interest. The reason for viewing this as an overstatement is in a way surprising: we learn something, although not very much, about the man's professional career and its requirements, but we are kept very uninformed about important segments of his private life.

Inheritance and Parents—Friends and Teachers

The personal relations of our heroes on which we are enlightened are, as a whole, limited to two groups, the parents and the friends. Both groups are taken in a specific sense: the parents comprising other older relations or forebears of former generations, the friends being more or less limited to people who were valuable in the hero's career. In more than half of the stories the father or the mother or the general family background is at least mentioned. Clark Gable's "stubborn determination" seems derived from his "Pennsylvania Dutch ancestors" (6); the very efficient State Department official, Mrs. Shipley, is the "daughter of a Methodist minister" (8); Senator Taft is a "middle-of-the-roader like his father," besides being "an aristocrat by birth and training" (101). We are let in a little bit on the family situation of Brenda Joyce because "somewhere there was a break-up between mamma and papa" (110). The general pattern of the parental home, however, is more on the Joan Carroll side, where we find the "young, quietly dignified mother . . . the successful engineer father . . . a star scout brother six years her senior" (143); we hear in a very sympathetic way about the old Fadimans, "the father a struggling Russian immigrant and pharmacist, the mother a nurse" (47); we learn a good deal about ancestors as in the case of Clark Gable cited above. Of the Secretary of Labor, Frances Perkins, we are told that her "forebears had settled all over New England between 1630 and 1680" (22); the female freighter skipper, D'Arcy Grant, has "an ancestral mixture of strongheaded swashbuckling Irish and pioneer Americans" (25); Raymond Gram Swing is the "heir of a severe New England tradition" (42); the Varian brothers have "Celtic blood" (52); in the woman matador, Conchita Cintron, we find "Spanish, Connecticut Irish, and Chilean elements" (116).

The curious fact here is not that the authors mention parentage, but that they have so much to say about it and so little to say about other human relations. It is a good deal as if the author wants to impress on the reader that his hero, to a very considerable extent, must be understood in terms of his biological and regional inheritance. It is a kind of primitive Darwinian concept of social facts: the tendency to place the burden of explanation and of responsibility on the shoulders of the past generations. The individual himself appears as a mere product of his past.

The element of passivity is also found in the second most frequently mentioned group of personal relationships: friends and teachers. Let us look again into some of the material. We hear that the woman diplomat,

Mrs. Harriman, was made "Minister to Norway because of her many powerful and loyal friends" (14); of the friendship between the hard-hit restaurateur, Johnson, and his wealthy doctor-friend (37); the movie actress, Brenda Marshall, was somehow saved in her career "by the friendship of a script girl" (161); Senator Byrnes got a good start because "a disillusioned old Charlestonian . . . showed him the ropes" (18); while Miss Perkins is " 'protected' by her personal secretary . . . [who] worships her" (22).

There is very rarely an episode that shows our heroes as active partners of friendship. In most cases their friends are their helpers. Very often they are teachers who later on become friends. Perhaps it is stretching a point to say that a vulgarian Darwinism is supplemented at this point by a vulgarian distortion of the "milieu" theory: the hero is a product of ancestry and friendship. But even if this may be somewhat exaggerated, it nevertheless helps to clarify the point, namely, that the hero appears in his human relationships as the one who takes, not as the one who gives.

We can supplement this statement by going back to our remark that decisive human relationships, and even those that are decisive for private lives, are missing. The whole sphere of the relations with the opposite sex is almost entirely missing. This is indeed a very strange phenomenon. We should assume that the predilection for such people as actors and actresses from stage and screen, night-club entertainers, etc., would be tied up with a special curiosity in such people's love affairs, but this is not the case at all. The realms of love, passion, even marriage, seem worth mentioning only in terms of vital statistics. It is quite a lot to be informed that Dorothy Thompson "got tangled up in love"; very soon Lewis "asked point black whether she would marry him" (9); Senator Byrnes "married the charming wife who still watches over him" (18); the industrial tycoon, Sloan, remarks, "Mrs. Sloan and I were married that summer . . . she was of Roxbury, Mass." (24); Mrs. Peabody married the rector "at the close of the school's first year" (29). We are told about Raymond Gram Swing only that he was married twice (42); as far as the bachelor situation of Lyons, the baseball player, goes, we hear that he "almost married his campus sweetheart" (53); while his colleague, Rizzuto, is "not even going steady" (57). In the high life of politics we are glad to know that Ambassador Lothian "gets on well with women" (115); and that Thomas Dewey is "a man's man, but women go for him" (117); we are briefly informed that Chris Martin "married, raised a family" (121); and that "one girl was sufficiently impressed to marry" Michael Todd, a producer, at the tender age of seventeen (131).

These statements of fact—in a matter-of-fact way, as, for instance, the mention of a marriage or a divorce— are all that we hear of that side of human relations that we were used to look upon as the most important ones. If we again imagine that these popular biographies should at a very distant historical moment serve as the sole source of information, the historian of the future would almost be forced to the conclusion that in our times the institution of marriage, and most certainly the phenomena of sexual passions, had become a very negligible factor. It seems that the fifth-rate role to which these phenomena are relegated fits very well with the emphasis on parentage and friendship. Love and passion require generosity, a display of productive mental and emotional forces that are neither primarily explained nor restrained by inheritance and advice.

A rather amusing observation: we found that the eyes of the hero were mentioned in almost one third of the stories. It is quite surprising that of all possible physiognomic and bodily features just this one should be so very popular. We take delight in the baseball umpire Bill Klem's "bright blue eyes," in his "even supernaturally good eyes" (104); or in the "modest brown eyes" of General Weygand (107). Miss Cintron, the matador, is "blue-eyed" (116); the night-club singer, Moffett, has "very bright blue eyes" (119).

We are not quite certain how to explain our biographers' bodily preferences. The eyes are commonly spoken of as "the windows of the soul." Perhaps it gratifies the more inarticulate reader if the authors let him try to understand the heroes in the same language in which he believes he understands his neighbor's soul. It is just another example of a cliché served up in lieu of a genuine attempt at psychological insight.

Home and Social Life—Hobbies and Food Preferences

The heroes, as we have seen, stem predominantly from the sphere of consumption and organized leisure time. It is fascinating to see how in the course of the presentation the producers and agents of consumer goods change into their own customers. Personal habits, from smoking to poker playing, from stamp collecting to cocktail parties, are faithfully noted in between 30 and 40 per cent of all stories under investigation. In fact, as soon as it comes to habits, pleasures, and distractions after and outside of working hours, the magazine biographer turns out to be just a snoopy reporter.

The politicians seem to be an especially ascetic lot— Taft "doesn't smoke" (101); neither does General Weygand (107); the former British Ambassador, Lothian, "hasn't taken a drink in 25 years" (115). There is also the movie actor, Chris Martin, who "doesn't smoke cigars or cigarettes" (121); the German Field Marshal Milch, whose "big black Brazilian cigars are his favored addiction" (146). To quote some of the favorite habits or dishes of the crowd: Dorothy Thompson is all out for "making Viennese dishes" while her "pet hates . . . are bungled broth and clumsily buttered tea bread" (9). We are invited to rejoice in Art Fletcher's "excellent digestion" (7). We hope that Major Angas is equally fortunate, for: "Eating well is his secondary career"; he is "perpetually hungry" (20). The circus magnate, North, also seems to have a highly developed sense for food and what goes with it: "His cud-cutters for a three-pound steak are a Martini, a Manhattan, and a beer, in that invariable order, tamped down with a hatful of radishes" (26).

As for the innocent hobbies of our heroes: Art Fletcher likes "the early evening movies" and also "to drive about the country" (7); Senator Byrnes finds recreation in "telling of the long saltily humorous anecdotes which all Southerners love" (18). The pitcher, Paige, is "an expert dancer and singer" (19); West-

brook Pegler "plays poker" (28); and his special pet
foe, Mayor Hague, also "likes gambling" (36); his
colleague, the London *Times* correspondent, Sir Willmott Lewis, also "plays poker" (49), while Swing takes
to badminton (42). More on the serious side is Greer
Garson, who "reads a great deal and studies the theater
every minute she is free" (113). The hobby of golf
unites Senator Taft (101), the fascist, Muti (114),
the "Blondie" cartoonist, Chic Young (165), the baseball player, Lyons (53), and Ambassador Lothian
(115).

We are furthermore told who likes to be "the life
of the party," and who does not; and also how the daily
routine in the apartment or private house is fixed. The
Flechers, for instance, "retire early and rise early" (7);
while Hank Greenberg "lives modestly with his parents" but also "likes night clubs, bright lights, and
pretty girls" (56). We hear of the actress Stickney's
charming "town house" (145), of the "fifteen rooms
and five baths and the private elevator to the street"
of political Boss Flynn (138); of the way in which the
ballet director Balanchine is "snugly installed in an
elaborate Long Island home, and a sleek New York
apartment" (152).

As to social gatherings: Nancy Hamilton's parties
"aren't glittering at all, but they are fun" (103). The
newspaperman, Silliman Evans, "has introduced the
Texas-size of large-scale outdoor entertainment" (39);
while his colleague, Clifton Fadiman, has "very little
social life, seldom goes to dinner parties" (47). His
habits seem related to those of the private island queen,
Jo Carstairs: ". . . A few friends of long standing

make up one of the world's shortest guest lists" (54).

And so it goes, through over two hundred quotations, changing a study in social relations into consumers' research. It is neither a world of "doers" nor a world of "doing" for which the biographical curiosity of a mass public is evoked. The whole trend goes toward acceptance: the biological and educational heritage; the helpful friends and teachers; the physical protection of the house, and the physiological one of eating and drinking; the security of social standing and prestige, through social entertaining; the complete resting of mind and work-wise energy through the gamut of hobbies. Here we come very close to decisive trends to which the modern individual seems subjected. He appears no longer as a center of outwardly bound energies and actions; as an inexhaustible reservoir of initiative and enterprise; no longer as an integral unity on whose work and efficiency might depend, not only his kin's future and happiness, but at the same time mankind's progress in general. Instead of the "givers" we are faced with the "takers." These new heroes represent a craving for having and taking things for granted. They seem to stand for a phantasmagoria of world-wide social security; for an attitude that asks for no more than to be served with the things needed for reproduction and recreation; for an attitude that has lost any primary interest in how to invent, shape, or apply the tools leading to such purposes of mass satisfaction.

We cannot avoid getting something of a distorted picture of society if we look at it exclusively through the personal lives of a few individuals. But in the past an effort was made to show the link between the hero and the nation's recent history. As one of those earlier biographers put it: "Each era, conscious of the mighty works that could be wrought, conscious that we are all under sentence of speedy death, eagerly seeks out the younger man, the obscure man. It has need of all powers and all talents. Especially of the talents for creating, organizing, and directing."[14]

Today the emphasis is on the routine functions of nourishment and leisure time and not on "the talents for creating, organizing, and directing." The real battlefield of history recedes from view or becomes a stock backdrop while society disintegrates into an amorphous crowd of consumers. Greer Garson and Mahatma Gandhi meet on common ground: the one "likes potatoes and stew and never tires of a breakfast of porridge and haddock" (113); the other's "evening meal is simple—a few dates, a little rice, goat's milk" (124); Hitler and Chris Martin "don't smoke . . ."

JUST FACTS

The quotation from Phillips can serve as a transition from the sociology of our heroes to their psychology. With its emphasis on the independence and leadership awaiting the exercise of personal initiative, it expresses the ideal character type of private capitalism.

There are at least two elements in this quotation, the presence of which characterizes the psychological

[14]D. G. Phillips, "The Right Hand to Pierpont Morgan," *Saturday Evening Post*, June 28, 1902.

concept of former biographies, and the absence of which is very meaningful for the present situation: development and solitude.

"The young, obscure man" has something of the heritage, however trivial in this case, of the personality as it was conceived during the rise of the middle-class culture: the individual as a totality of potentialities, mental, moral, and emotional, which have to be developed in a given social framework. Development, as the essence of human life, was connected with the idea that the individual has to find himself in the soliloquy of the mind. Human existence seemed to be made up of the loneliness of the creature and of his emergence into the outer world by displaying his own gifts. Our quotation is one of the late forms of this concept: the self-developing and fighting individual with all the chances in the world for creation and conquest.

Souls without History

In an essay on present-day man Max Horkheimer states: "Development has ceased to exist."[15] His remarks on the immediate transition from childhood to adult life, his observation that "the child is grown up as soon as he can walk, and the grown-up in principle always remains the same," sound as if they were a comment on our biographical heroes. Among our quotations we have a collection of passages that try to tie up the childhood of the hero with his later life. Almost every second story brings some report on the road from childhood to maturity. Does this not seem to contra-

[15]Max Horkheimer, "The End of Reason," *Studies in Philosophy and Social Science*, 9:3 (1941), 381.

dict our general remark, is this not a variation of the classical concept of the emerging personality? Before answering let us examine a few representative passages: At the age of twelve "wrestling . . . was the answer to my problem," says the wrestler, Allman (13). The king of horse-race betting, Pittsburgh Phil, "began betting when he was fourteen—on his own game chickens" (23). Of the inventor, Stout, it is remarked: "Wherever his family lived, he would rig up a crude shop and try to make things" (41). At twelve the future actor, Ezra Stone, ran a kids' program "directing the actors and paying them off at the end of the week" (108). For the Ringling-Barnum head, J. R. North, "a real circus was his toy" (26). The future film star, Greer Garson, "wanted to be an actress from the time she could walk" (113). The night-club singer Hildegarde's parents "weren't surprised when Hildegarde, . . . aged eighteen months, hummed a whole aria of an opera they had carried her to" (135).

Childhood appears neither as prehistory and key to the character of an individual nor as a stage of transition to the growth and formation of the abundant diversity of an adult. Childhood is nothing but a midget edition, a predated publication of a man's profession and career. A man is an actor, a doctor, a dancer, an entrepreneur, and he always was. He was not born the tender and unknown potentiality of a human life, of an intellectual, mental, emotional creativeness, effective for himself and for society; rather he came into the world and stayed in it, rubber-stamped with and for a certain function. The individual has become a trademark.

In more than a third of the stories an attempt at a "theory of success" seems to be made, but no magic formula is offered that an average individual might follow for his own good. The bulk of the answers consists of more or less trivial suggestions that the key may be found in "instinct" or other vague qualities. The golf player, Bobby Jones, "must have been born with the deep love for the game" (11). As to the Senator: "Leadership is Byrnes' real genius" (18). Pittsburgh Phil was "a good horse player by instinct" (23). The achievements of the football coach, Kendrigan, are a mystery even to him: "how he did it he never figured" (50). The air-line tycoon, Cyrus R. Smith, may count on "an unerring gambler's instinct" (51). This key formula of instinct is supplemented by a collection of almost tautological truisms: The fascist, Muti, "loves his danger highly spiced" (114). The sociable ambassador, Lothian, "likes newspapermen" (115). Howard Johnson knows what makes a restaurant successful: "A man that is properly supervised never goes haywire" (37). And as far as Clark Gable's success is concerned (and this could be applied to all the 125) "The answer . . . is personality" (6).

We venture to interpret this pseudo-psychology of success as another aspect of the timeless and passive image of modern man. Just as childhood is an abbreviation of the adult's professional career, so is the explanation of this career nothing but an abstract, rather inarticulate reiteration that a career is a career and a success is a success.

The psychological atmosphere breathes behaviorism on a very primitive level. Childhood as well as that vague realm of instincts represent, so to speak, the biological background from which a variety of human qualities emerge. It is a psychology that shows no need of asking why and, precisely in the same sense in which we tried to show it for sociology, testifies to the transformation from the worship of a spontaneous personality to the adoration of an existence shaped and molded by outside forces. These people live in a limbo of children and victims. The way leads to what we are inclined to call "a command psychology" because people are not conceived as the responsible agents of their fate in all phases of their lives, but as the bearers of certain useful or not so useful character traits that are pasted on them like decorations or stigmas of shame.

There are a few traits that seem to have some bearing on a man's ability to manipulate his environment. We mean the columnist who is a "spotlight stealer" (9); the playwright-actress who never overlooks "good spots for herself" (103); the producer who is "his own ballyhoo artist" (131). We mean the baseball manager who is "chemically opposed to being on the sucker end of a ball game" (2); the smart nightclub star who sees "no point in disclosing that King Gustave's favorite singer had been born over her father's delicatessen store" (135); the actress who has real "talent for meeting people" (103); the person who shows up "at the right place at the right time" (109); who is a "great man in flying, handshaking and backslapping trips" (21).

The majority of such attitudes are likely to evoke a slyly understanding smile on the part of the observer and reader. These are the "sure-fire" tricks on the road to success, a little doubtful, but not too bad; these are the equipment of the shrewd man and the smart woman. But these psychological gadgets exhaust the list of qualities pertaining to creative and productive abilities. They generate an atmosphere of pseudo-creativeness in an attempt to convince us that a man has contributed his personal, individual share to the general cause of progress. "Something new has been added," insists the advertisement, but beware of inquiring too closely into the nature of the novelty. Thus, the good-natured statements of a certain lack of meticulous innocence on the road to success become for the sociological interpreter a sad revelation of a lack of originality in productive strength.

This is brought out even more clearly when we turn to the presentation of the actual history of success. Here success is not even attributed to some happy instinct—it merely happens. Success has lost the seductive charm that once seemed to be a promise and a prize for everybody who was strong, clever, flexible, sober enough to try. It has become a rigid matter on which we look with awe or envy as we look at the priceless pictures in our galleries or the fabulous palaces of the rich. The success of our heroes of consumption is in itself goods of consumption. It does not serve as an instigator for more activity; it is introduced as something we have to accept just like the food and drink and the parties; it is nourishment for curiosity and entertainment.

The mythology of success in the biographies consists of two elements, hardship and breaks. The troubles and difficulties with which the road to success is paved are discussed in the form of stereotypes. Over and over again we hear that the going is rough and hard. The baseball umpire goes "the long, rough road up to that night of triumph" (104); the lightweight champion "came up the hard way" (123); a Senator knew in his youth the "long hours of hard work" (149); and the ballet director "worked hard" (152). In identical words we hear that the baseball manager (2) and the great film star (6) "came up the hard way." The "hard way" it was for Dorothy Thompson (9) and for Billy Rose (43). We are reminded of official military communiqués, reporting a defeat or stalemate in a matter-of-fact tone, rather than descriptions of life processes.

The same applies to the reverse side of hardship: to the so-called breaks. All our stories refer to successes and it is fair enough that somehow we must be informed when and how the failures stopped. Here the tendency to commute life data into facts to be accepted rather than understood becomes intensified. Usually the beginning of the peak is merely stated as an event: A high civil servant was "fortunate in her first assignment" (8); a cartoonist merely gets a "telegram offering him a job on the paper," which later leads to his fame (34); a radio commentator "bursts into certain popularity" (42); an actor "got a break" (112); another "got the job and it turned out well" (121); for a middleweight champion "the turning point of his career had arrived" (142). If any explanation is offered at all, we are told that the turn occurred in some freakish way: the night-club singer gets started by "a king's whim" (135); Clark Gable's appointment as a time-keeper with a telephone company appears as the turning point in his career (6); a baseball player goes on a fishing trip, loses his old job, and thereby gets another one, which leads to his success (133a).

These episodes of repetition and freakishness seem to demonstrate that there is no longer a social pattern for the way up. Success has become an accidental and irrational event. The dangers of competition were tied up with the idea of definite chances and there was a sound balance between ambition and possibilities. Appropriately enough, our heroes are almost without ambition, a tacit admission that those dangers of the past have been replaced by the cruelties of the present. It is cruel, indeed, that the ridiculous game of chance should open the doors to success for a handful, while all the others who were not present when it happened are failures. The "facts" of a career are a reflection of the lack of spontaneity. Behind the amusing, fortuitious episode lurks a terrible truth.[16] Hardships and breaks are standard articles for the reader. They are just a better brand of what everyone uses. The outstanding has become the proved specimen of the average. By impressing on the reading masses the idols of our civilization, any criticism or even reasoning about the validity of such standards is suppressed. As a social

[16]The spectacle of success, hardships, and accidents is attended in the biographies by an assortment of numbers and figures that purport to bestow glamor and exactness to the narration. Calculability is the ideal language of modern biographies. They belong to the scientific mentality, that sees its ideal in the transformation from quality into quantity. Life's riddle is solved if caught in a numeric constellation. The majority of figures refer to income, to which may be added relatively few data on capital. The other figures pertain to the spectators of a ball game, to the budget of a city, to the votes of an election, etc.

scientist the biographer represents a pitiless, almost sadistic trend in science, for he demonstrates the recurring nature of such phenomena as hardships and breaks, but he does not attempt to reveal the laws of such recurrence. For him knowledge is not the source of power, but merely the key to adjustment.

Catalogue of Adjustment

When we turn to a study of the approval and disapproval our authors attach to the various character traits they describe, we find a striking and simple pattern.

In tone the catalogue of these traits, like the mythology of success, resembles a digest of military orders of the day: brusque laudations and reprimands. There is no room for nuances or ambiguity. In content it is on a very simple level and the criterion of approval or disapproval is also very simple. The yardstick is social adjustment. Once we realize the subconscious and conscious opinions of present-day society on what an adjusted person should or should not be, we are thoroughly familiar with the evaluation of character traits and their owners. The yardstick has three scales: behavior toward material tasks; behavior toward fellow men; and behavior in relation to one's own emotions. The one who is efficient scores in the first sphere; the one who is sociable, in the second; the one who is always restrained, in the third.

In a separate study of all passages mentioning character traits, we found that of a total of seventy-six quotations referring to a hero's commendable behavior toward "things to be done" not fewer than seventy, or over 90 per cent, mentioned competence, efficiency, and energy; the remaining six referred to ambition. The majority read: "very capable" (154); "no sacrifice of time, effort, or my own convenience was too great" (24); "an inordinately hard worker" (48); "was never fired for inefficiency" (167); "thorough and accurate" (16); "being idle is her idea of complete torture" (140).

Out of a total of forty-eight quotations mentioning commendable behavior in relation to people all forty-eight quote "co-operation," "sociability," and "good sportsmanship." There is a constant repetition of such adjectives as "co-operative," "generous," and "sociable." A baseball manager is "easy to meet, sociable, unsparing in his time with interviewers" (27). The "sociable" chief of the Passport Division (8); the Secretary of Labor, "a delightful hostess" (22); the Republican candidate for the presidency with his "liking for and interest in people" (133); the matador, "genial, friendly, hospitable" (116); a smart actress, "amiable and friendly" (140)—they all belong to one big happy family which knows no limits in being pleasant and agreeable to each other. Like Don James, the barker for sideshows, they all seem to have "hearts huge and overflowing" (127).

The number of quotations pertaining to disapproved character traits is very small, but conspicuous among them are criticisms of the unrestrained expression of emotion. It is virtually horrible that one of our baseball heroes "is no man for a jest when losing a game" (53); that a movie actress "cannot bear to be teased" (105); or that our Secretary of Labor's "public relations are unfortunate" (22). Unrestrained behavior traits like being "irritable and harsh" (32), "swift, often furious testiness" (117), being "unbalanced" (56), or even possessing a "somewhat difficult personality" (117) are really most unpleasant. Such faults can be tolerated only if they are exceptional—like the man who "for once got his feelings beyond control" (23).

The catalogue of normalcy leaves no room for individuality. This catalogue levels human behavior by the rejection of emotional eruptions; the bad marks given to the poor "joiners" and the temperamental people; the complete lack of creative and passionate behavior among the commendable qualities. The absence of love and passion in our catalogue of human relations finds its counterpart in this catalogue of human qualities. It is a world of dependency. The social implications of such atmosphere seem to be considerable because in their social status the majority of our heroes are either their "own boss" or they have climbed to such a high step in the social ladder that whole worlds separate them from the average employee. Yet the few "big ones" do not differ basically from the many little ones. They demonstrate, taken as a group, not the exception, but the typical cross-section of the sociopsychological condition of modern society.

The foregoing examples from our catalogue of character traits should make clear why we emphasize the double feature of the absence of development and solitude. The average man is never alone and never wants to be alone. His social and psychological birth is the community, the masses. His human destiny seems to be a life of continuous adjustment: adjustment to the world through efficiency and industriousness; and adjustment to people by exhibiting amiable and sociable qualities and by repressing all other traits. There is no religious or philosophical framework according to which the character traits are classified and evaluated. The concepts of good and bad, of kindness and sin, of truth and falsehood, of sacrifice and selfishness, of love and hate are not the beacons that illuminate our human landscape. The character image on which an affirmative judgment is passed in the biographies is that of a well-trained employee from a well-disciplined lower-middle-class family. Our people could occupy an imaginary world of technocracy; everybody seems to reflect a rigid code of flexible qualities: the rigid and mechanized setup of a variety of useful mechanical institutions. Behind the polished mask of training and adjustment lurks the concept of a human robot who, without having done anything himself, moves just such parts and in just such directions as the makers wished him to do.

Formerly it was only the sick who needed handling because it was known that their symptoms were similar to many others. Now everyone is reduced to the same dependency. The pride of being an individual with his own very personal ways and interests becomes the stigma of abnormality. Interest in the consumption of others is an expression of lack of interest in genuine consumption. The detailed character description is dominated by the same acceptance and passivity that came to the foreground in the concept of souls without development.

LANGUAGE

Superlatives

Our analysis would not be complete without some discussion of our stories' language, which has several characteristic features. The most obvious one is the superlative.[17] Once we are made aware of this stylistic device, it cannot be overlooked. The heroes themselves, their accomplishments and experiences, their friends and acquaintances are characterized as unique beings and events. The superlative gives a good conscience to the biographer—by applying a rhetorical gadget he achieves the transformation of the average into the extraordinary. Mr. Muti is "the toughest fascist of them all" (114); Dr. Brinkley is the "best advertised doctor in the United States" (3); our hero is the "luckiest man in the movies today" (121); another is "not only the greatest, but the first real showman in the Ringling family" (26). There is a general who is "one of the best mathematicians this side of Einstein" (107). There is a columnist with "one of the strangest of courtships" (9); another statesman with "the world's most exciting job" (144). There are also the downward-pointed superlatives. Some sportsman was once "the loudest and by all odds the most abusive of the

[17]An unpublished study of this writer on popular German biographies in book form shows that the use of superlatives also characterizes them. These books by Emil Ludwig, Stefan Zweig, and others are on a different intellectual level, yet it seems probable that similar sociological implications hold for them as for magazine biographies.

100

lot" (2); a newspaperman is "one of the most consistently resentful men in the country" (28); another person is "one of the unhappiest women that ever lived" (154).

As if the biographer had to convince himself and his public that he is really selling an excellent human specimen, he sometimes is not satisfied with the ratio of one superlative per sentence, but has to pack a lot of them into a single passage. Pittsburgh Phil is "the most famous and the most feared horse player in America" (23). The German Labor Front is "the best led, most enlightened and most powerful labor organization in Europe" (21). The producer, Lorentz, "demands the best writing, the best music and the best technical equipment available" (126). The baseball manager, Clark Griffith, "was the most colorful star on the most colorful team in baseball" (2). Tilden is ". . . the greatest tennis player in the world and the greatest guy in the world" (111).

This whole distribution of highest ratings defeats its own purpose. Everything is presented as something unique, unheard of, outstanding. Thus nothing is unique, unheard of, outstanding. Totality of the superlative means totality of the mediocre. It levels the presentation of human life to the presentation of merchandise. The most vivacious girl corresponds to the best toothpaste, the highest endurance in sportsmanship corresponds to the most efficient vitamins; the unique performance of the politician corresponds to the unsurpassed efficiency of the automobile. There is a pre-established harmony between the objects of mass production in the advertising columns and the objects of biography in the editorial comment. The language of promotion has replaced the language of evaluation. Only the price tag is missing.

The superlative pushes the reader between two extremes. He is graciously attempting to become conversant with people who are paragons of human accomplishment. He may be proud that to a great extent these wonderful people do nothing but entertain him. He has, at least in his leisure time, the best crowd at his fingertips. But there is no road left to him for an identification with the great, or for an attempt to emulate their success. Thus the superlative, like the story of success itself, brings out the absence of those educational features and other optimistic implications that were characteristic of biographies during the era of liberalism. What on first sight seems to be the rather harmless atmosphere of entertainment and consumption is, on closer examination, revealed as a reign of psychic terror, where the masses have to realize the pettiness and insignificance of their everyday life. The already weakened consciousness of being an individual is struck another heavy blow by the pseudo-individualizing forces of the superlative. Advertisement and terror, invitation to entertainment and summons to humility form their unity in the world of superlatives. The biographer performs the functions of a side-show barker for living attractions and of a preacher of human insignificance.

High and Low Language

The use of the superlative is reinforced by frequent references to an assortment of mythical and historical

associations, in order, it would seem, to confer pseudo-
sanctity and pseudo-safety to the futile affairs of modern mass culture. Clark Gable does not just make a
career—he lives the "Gable saga" (6), and the movie
actress, Joyce, experiences at least a "little saga" (110).
"Historic" is the word for Ilka Chase (140) as well as
for Hildegarde (135). What happens to the softball
player Novikoff is "fabulous" (158); the fate of the
actress Morison is "history" (162); of the movie producer Wallis (166) as well as of the ball player Allen
(45) "a miracle"; the baseball manager Griffith experiences "baseball destiny," he accomplishes "a historic
piece of strategy" (2). Greek mythology is a favorite;
Clark Gable lives in "Olympian regions" (6); the passport administrator Shipley (8) as well as the gadget
inventor Taylor (167) have a "Herculean task"; the
producer Todd is called an "Archon" (131) and our
Taylor "Orpheus" (167). Of course Christianity and
the Middle Ages have to help Dorothy Thompson "like
a knight with a righteous sword" (9); the nazi Ley is
the "Jacob of German labor" with "labor itself the Esau"
(21). Vice-President Wallace is "Joseph, a dreamer of
dreams" (38); Casals is a "good samaritan" (106). There
are no limits. Ruth Hussey sometimes "looked a bit like
a Buddha" (151); the showman Rose like a "priest of
Osiris" (43). And so it goes on with myths, legends,
sagas, destinies, miracles.[18] And yet, in the same breath

[18]Helen McGill Hughes, *op. cit.*, p. 183, is aware of the fact
that the association of "classical" names has a stimulating effect
on what she calls "the city demos": "Stated in terms of his
popular literature, the mind of modern man lives in the present.
And as the present changes, so his news is voluminous and
rapidly succeeded by more news. But what fascinates him is the

that bestows the blessings of venerable symbols on our heroes they and we are brought together on the easy level of slang and colloquial speech. McCutcheon, the cartoonist, might be called the "king" of his island possession, but we hear that "kingship is a safe investment" (1); Fletcher, who made history, is also "the soul—or the heel—of honesty" (7); Swing, called "an apostle," has also "radio's best bedside manner" (42). When Taft's father was president, the "crown of Roosevelt I fitted him like a five and ten toupee" (101). There is a boxer who finds it "good business to be brave" (12); there is "gossip—a dime a gross" (23); there is talk of a "personal blitzkrieg" (29); of "votes enough to elect a bee to a beehive" (109); of "that genius business" (152). The historizing hymns of praise and transfiguration correspond to movie "palaces" and the sport "stadiums." Behind the façade of language there rules, just as behind the architectural outside make-up, a versatility of techniques, gadgets, and tricks for which nothing is too expensive or too cheap that may serve the purpose of entertaining or being entertained.

These substitutes and successors of creative production require a language that substitutes for elucidat-

---

news story—the true story—even though it may duplicate *Bluebeard* or *Romeo and Juliet* so exactly that the headline tells the news just by mentioning the familiar names. The human interest of the common man in the modern world will, and does, ensnare him into reading folk tales or even the classics, dull and unreal as he finds them in themselves, if they are paraphrased as the careers of twentieth-century Electras, Macbeths and a Moll Flanders, for he is preoccupied with the things that depart from the expected and make news."

ing, revealing, stimulating words a linguistic confusion that strives to produce the illusion of rooted tradition and all-around alertness. Thus this new literary phenomenon complies with the highest artistic criteria: inner, necessary, inseparable connection between form and content, between expression and the expressed—in short, a linguistic creation that will not permit an anatomic clear-cut separation between words and their intentions! These biographies as a literary species are "true."

Especially for You

In an unpublished analysis of songs T. W. Adorno interprets the pseudo-directness with which every one of the millions of girls for whose consumption the hit is manufactured seems to be addressed. The pseudo-individualization of the heroes corresponds to the pseudo-individualization of the readers. Although the selection of heroes and what is reported about them are as thoroughly standardized as the language of these reports, there is the superlative functioning as the specifying agent for the chosen hero and there is also, as crown and conclusion, the direct speech as the bearer of a personal message to the reader. Affably or condescendingly everyone is personally invited to attend the spectacle of an outstanding life. Individual meets individual; the biographer takes care of the introduction.

Coach Fletcher and his wife "can be reached only by telegram provided you know the address" (7). Should you happen to be a Brenda Joyce fan: "If you come at the right time, you will see her second-hand car" (110). Watching our election campaign: "If Hull and Mr. Taft are the candidates, your emotion will not be fired, nor will your sleep be disturbed by them" (109). For those interested in film stars: "Let's sit down with Bill Powell and listen to his story" (112); "perhaps, girls, you would like to know how Clark Gable got that way" (6). Reporting McCutcheon's acquisition of an island, the author teases the reader: "so, you want to be a king" (1). For the car owner: "You can't help seeing Johnson's restaurants if you drive along main highways" (37). There is the London *Times* representative Sir Willmott Lewis: "Meet him on Pennsylvania Avenue. He will stop and talk to you as if you were a five hundred audience" (49). Umpire Klem "knows the multitudinous rules of baseball better than you know the alphabet" (104). Let there be no mistake: the night club singer Moffett "went to the very best schools, my dear" (119). But let's not neglect her colleague Hildegarde: "If you haven't heard her or seen her, don't stand there—go, do something about it" (135). Casals' biographer is a little less imperative: "Meet the blond bowman from Spain" (106). Dependability is the word for Miss Fitzgerald: ". . . you can bank on her for the truth" (105).

The direct apostrophe is similar in function to the superlative: it creates elation and humiliation. The reader, besides being admitted to the intimate details of the hero's habits in eating, spending, playing, has the pleasure of personal contact. There is nothing of the measured distance and veneration that a reader in the classics in biography had to observe before the statesman of the past, or the poet or the scientist. The aristocracy of a gallery of isolated bearers of unusual achievements seems to be replaced by a democratic meeting which requires no special honors and genuflection before the great.

But the ease of admission is not devoid of menacing features. The "You" means, not only the friendly gesture of introduction, but also the admonishing, calling voice of a superior agency, proclaiming that one has to observe, has to comply. The language of directness betrays the total coverage planned by all modern institutions of mass communication. "Especially for You" means all of you.

THE READER

Magazine biographers have undergone a process of expansion as well as of atrophy. They have become a standard institution in magazines that count their audience by the millions. But the scope of this expanding world of biographies has been narrowed down to the highly specialized field of entertainment. If we ask again what social need they serve, we might find the answer in this combination of quantitative increase and qualitative deterioration.

A hypothesis on the pseudo-educational and pseudo-scientific function of the popular biography can be formulated as follows: the task of the social scientist is, in very broad terms, the clarification of the hidden processes and interconnections of social phenomena. The average reader who, like an earnest and independent student, is not satisfied with a mere conglomeration of facts or concepts, but wants to know what it is all about, seems to gain insight from these biographies, and an understanding of the human or social secret of the historical process. But this is only a trick, because these individuals whose lives he studies are neither characteristic of this process nor are they presented in such a way that they appear in the full light of it. A rather satisfactory understanding of the reader is possible if we look upon the biography as an agent of make-believe adult education. A certain social prestige, the roots of which are planted during one's school days, constantly drives one toward higher values in life, and specifically toward more complete knowledge. But these biographies corrupt the educational conscience by delivering goods that bear an educational trademark but are not the genuine article.

The important role of familiarity in all phenomena of mass culture cannot be sufficiently emphasized. People derive a great deal of satisfaction from the continual repetition of familiar patterns. There are but a very limited number of plots and problems, which are repeated over and over again in successful movies and short stories; even the so-called exciting moments in sports events are to a great extent very much alike. Everyone knows that he will hear more or less the same type of story and the same type of music as soon as he turns on the radio. But there has never been any rebellion against this fact; there has never been a psychologist who could have said that boredom characterized the faces of the masses when they participate in the routine pleasures. Perhaps, since the average working day follows a routine that often does not show any change during a lifetime, the routine and repetition characteristics of leisure-time activities serve as a kind of justification and glorification of the working day. They appear in the guise of beauty and pleasure when they rule, not only during the average day, but also in the average late afternoon and evening. In our biographies the horizon is not extended to the realm of the unknown, but is instead painted with the figures of the known. We have already seen the movie actor performing on the screen and we have seen the cartoons of the competent newspaperman; we have heard what the radio commentator has to say and have noted the talents of boxers and baseball players. The biographies repeat what we have always known.

André Maurois has made a wrong prophecy: "We shall come once more into periods of social and religious certainty in which few intimate biographies will be written and *panegyrics* will take their place. Subsequently we shall again reach a period of doubt and despair in which biographies will reappear as a source of confidence and reassurance."[19] The reader who obviously cherishes the duplication of being entertained with the life stories of his entertainers must have an irrepressible urge to get something in his mind that he can really hold fast and fully understand. It has been said of reading interests that: "In general, so long as the things of fundamental importance are not presenting one with problems, one scarcely attends to

[19]André Maurois, *Aspects of Biography*, Appleton-Century, New York, 1939, p. 203.

them in any way.[20] This remark has an ironical connotation for our biographies, for it can hardly be said that "things of importance" are not presenting us with problems today. Yet they are scarcely attended to unless we would admit that our heroes' parents, their likes and dislikes in eating and playing, and, in the majority of cases, even their professions are important data during the initial stages of World War II. But the distance between what an average individual may do and the forces and powers that determine his life and death has become so unbridgeable that identification with normalcy, even with Philistine boredom, becomes a readily grasped empire of refuge and escape. It is some comfort for the little man who has become expelled from the Horatio Alger dream, who despairs of penetrating the thicket of grand strategy in politics and business, to see his heroes as a lot of guys who like or dislike highballs, cigarettes, tomato juice, golf, and social gatherings—just like himself. He knows how to converse in the sphere of consumption and here he can make no mistakes. By narrowing his focus of attention he can experience the gratification of being confirmed in his own pleasures and discomforts by participating in the pleasures and discomforts of the great. The large confusing issues in the political and economic realm and the antagonisms and controversies in the social realm—all these are submerged in the experience of being at one with the lofty and great in the sphere of consumption.

[20]Franklin Bobbitt, "Major Fields of Human Concern," quoted in: Gray and Munroe, *op. cit.*, p. 47.

APPENDIX

If we study the professional distribution for the two magazines separately we find the following result:

TABLE 4. Distribution of Biographical Subjects by Occupation in *The Saturday Evening Post* and *Collier's* from April 1940 to April 1941

Occupations of subjects	The Saturday Evening Post		Collier's	
	No.	%	No.	%
Politics	16	28	15	22
Business and professions	20	35	5	7
Entertainment, sports ..	20	37	49	71
Total	56	100	69	100

This table shows a considerable difference between *The Saturday Evening Post* and *Collier's* in the occupational distribution of heroes. There are far more "serious" people and far fewer entertainers in *The Saturday Evening Post*. This corresponds to a difference in the audiences of the two magazines. Surveys have shown that the average *Saturday Evening Post* reader is older, wealthier, and more attached to his home and more interested in social and economic problems than the average reader of *Collier's*.[21]

However, the difference between the two magazines becomes negligible (see Table 5) when we reclassify the heroes according to the spheres of politics, production, and consumption. For our purpose this is a more meaningful classification. As the two magazines are rather alike under this classification we felt justified in treating them together in the main text.

[21] *A Qualitative Study of Magazines: Who Reads Them and Why*. McCall Corporation, October 1939.

TABLE 5. Distribution of Biographical Subjects by General Spheres of Activity in *The Saturday Evening Post* and *Collier's* from April 1940 to April 1941

Spheres	The Saturday Evening Post		Collier's	
	No.	%	No.	%
Politics	16	28	15	22
Production	3	5	..	..
Consumption	37	67	54	78
Total	56	100	69	100

We give below the list of the biographies from *The Saturday Evening Post* and *Collier's* appearing in the issues between April 1940 and April 1941.

The Saturday Evening Post

Date	"Hero"	Profession	No.
4-6-40...........	John T. McCutcheon	Cartoonist	1
4-13, 20-40.......	Clark Griffith	Baseball manager	2
4-20-40...........	John R. Brinkley	Physician	3
5-4-40...........	Robert Taft	Senator	4
5-4-40...........	Jack Johnson	Boxer	5
5-4-40...........	Clark Gable	Movie actor	6
5-11-40...........	Art Fletcher	Baseball coach	7

Date	"Hero"	Profession	No.
10–12–40	James C. Petrillo	President, American Federation of Musicians	32
10–12–40	Louis McHenry Howe	Presidential secretary	33
10–19–40	Jay Norwood Darling	Cartoonist	34
10–19–40	Sidney Hillman	Labor leader	35
10–26–40	Frank Hague	Mayor of Jersey City	36
11–2–40	Howard Johnson	Owner of a restaurant chain	37
11–2–40	Henry Wallace	Vice-President	38
11–23–40	Silliman Evans	Newspaperman	39
11–30–40	Jesse H. Jones	Secretary of Commerce	40
12–7–40	William B. Stout	Inventor	41
12–14–40	Raymond Gram Swing	Radio commentator	42
12–21–40	Billy Rose	Showman	43
12–28–40	Charles A. Lindbergh	Aviator, etc.	44
12–28–40	Bobby Allen	Ball player	45
1–4–41	Toto	A gorilla	46
1–11–41	Clifton Fadiman	Book and radio critic	47
1–18–41	Sam Rayburn	Speaker, House of Representatives	48
1–25–41	Sir Willmott Lewis	London *Times* emissary to U.S.	49
2–1–41	J. H. Kendrigan	Football coach	50
2–1–41	Cyrus R. Smith	Pres. Amer. Airlines	51
2–8–41	Varian brothers	Inventors	52
2–15–41	Theodore A. Lyons	Baseball player	53
2–22–41	Jo Carstairs	Island proprietress	54
3–8, 15–41	Preston Sturges	Movie writer and director	55

3-15-41	Hank Greenberg	Baseball player	56
3-22-41	Phil Rizzuto	Baseball player	57

Collier's

4-6-40	Robert A. Taft	Senator	101
4-13-40	Mme. Chao Wu-Tang	Chinese partisan chief	102
4-13-40	Nancy Hamilton	Playwright, actress	103
4-13-40	Bill Klem	Baseball umpire	104
4-20-40	Geraldine Fitzgerald	Movie actress	105
4-20-40	Pablo Casals	Cellist	106
4-27-40	General Weygand	General	107
4-27-40	Ezra Stone	Stage, radio and screen actor	108
5-4-40	Cordell Hull	Secretary of State	109
5-4-40	Brenda Joyce	Movie actress	110
5-4-40	Bill Tilden	Tennis champion	111
5-11-40	William Powell	Movie actor	112
5-18-40	Greer Garson	Movie actress	113
5-25-40	Ettore Muti	Fascist politician	114
5-25-40	Philip Kerr, Marquess of Lothian	British Ambassador	115
5-25-40	Conchita Cintron	Woman matador	116
6-8-40	Thomas Dewey	Politician	117
6-8-40	Athanasiades	Munitions merchant	118
6-15-40	Adelaide Moffett	Night-club entertainer	119
6-22-40	Dutch Leonard	Baseball player	120
6-22-40	Chris Martin	Movie actor	121

Date	"Hero"	Profession	No.
6-29-40	Gene Tierney	Movie actress	122
7-20-40	Lew Jenkins	Lightweight champion	123
7-20-40	Mahatma Gandhi	Indian political leader	124
7-27-40	Jean Arthur	Movie actress	125
8-3-40	Pare Lorentz	Movie producer	126
8-10-40	Don James	Side-show barker	127
8-24-40	Larry Adler	Harmonica player	128
8-31-40	Ernest Bevin	British Minister of Labor	129
9-7-40	Helen Bernhard	Tennis player	130
9-7-40	Mike Todd	Producer–show business	131
9-14-40	Ingrid Bergman	Movie actress	132
9-21-40	Wendell Willkie	Politician	133
9-28-40	Walters and Derringer	Baseball players	133a
10-5-40	Juan March	Industrialist	134
10-5-40	Hildegarde	Night-club singer	135
10-12-40	Jack Grain	Football player	136
10-12-40	Jinx Falkenburg	Advertising model	137
10-12-40	Eddie Flynn	Democratic National Chairman	138
10-19-40	John Latouche	Writer	139
10-26-40	Ilka Chase	Actress—movie, radio	140
11-2-40	Winston Churchill	British Prime Minister	141
11-2-40	Ken Overlin	Middleweight champion	142
11-9-40	Joan Carroll	Child movie actress	143
11-9-40	Lord Woolton	Britain's Minister of Food	144
11-16-40	Dorothy Stickney	Actress—theater	145

Suggestions for Further Reading

BERNARD BERELSON AND MORRIS JANOWITZ. *Reader in Public Opinion and Communication* (Glencoe, Illinois: Free Press, 1953). A large number of articles and a full bibliography.

BERNARD BERELSON AND PATRICIA SALTER. "Majority and Minority Americans: An Analysis of Magazine Fiction," *Public Opinion Quarterly*, 10:2 (Summer 1946), 168–90. "A study of the unintentional but consistent prejudice against minority groups" in popular magazine fiction.

ORRIN E. KLAPP. "The Creation of Popular Heroes," *American Journal of Sociology*, 54:2 (September 1948), 135–41; "Hero Worship in America," *American Sociological Review*, 14:1 (February 1949), 53–62. Suggestive analyses of the hero as a social type.

DAVID RIESMAN, NATHAN GLAZER, AND REUEL DENNEY, *The Lonely Crowd: A Study of the Changing American Character* (New York: Doubleday Anchor, 1955). Analyzes in more general terms the shift from production to consumption as the main concern of Americans.

The People's Choice

PAUL F. LAZARSFELD, BERNARD BERELSON,
& HAZEL GAUDET

This is a report on modern American political behavior—specifically on the formation of votes during
a presidential campaign. Briefly, our problem was to
discover how and why people decided to vote as they
did, and for this purpose we used the so-called panel
technique: *repeated interviewing of the same people.*

In May 1940 every fourth house in Erie County, Ohio,
was visited by a member of a staff of from twelve to fifteen specially trained local interviewers, chiefly women.
From this "poll" of 3000, four groups of 600 persons
each were selected by stratified sampling. Each group
was closely matched to the others and constituted, in
effect, a miniature sample of the county. Of these four
groups of 600 three were reinterviewed only once each
—one in July, one in August, and one in October. They
were used as "control groups" to test the effect that
repeated interviewing might have on the panel. The
fourth group—the panel—was interviewed once each
month from May to November.

Whenever a person changed his vote intention in
any way from one interview to the next, detailed infor-

mation was gathered on why he had changed. The respondents were also interviewed regularly on their exposure to campaign propaganda in all the media of communication—the press, radio, personal contacts, and others. In addition, the repeated interviews made it possible to secure information about each respondent's personal characteristics, social philosophy, political history, personality traits, relations with other people, opinions on issues related to the election—in short, information on anything that might contribute to our knowledge of the formation of his political preferences.

Erie County, Ohio, 1940

Erie County, located on Lake Erie between Cleveland and Toledo, was chosen because it was small enough to permit close supervision of the interviewers, because it was relatively free from sectional peculiarities, because it was not dominated by any large urban center although it did furnish an opportunity to compare rural political opinion with opinion in a small urban center, and because for forty years—in every presidential election in the twentieth century—it had deviated very little from the national voting trends.

The population of Erie County in 1940 was 43,000, almost all native-born white. The people were largely of the working class, with a sprinkling of upper-class merchants, manufacturers, and professional men. They depended on simple things for pleasures. The family was an important social unit (and political as well, as we shall see later). Sandusky, the county seat, was known as a "church town" and the church was often the core of social life. Each church had a wide range of organizations for men, women, and children. The preachers were conservative: they preached the gospel and did not participate much in civic or political affairs. Fraternal and business groups were normally active, as were the usual forum and discussion groups. The school system was manned by competent, progressive, non-partisan elements. The Catholic Church maintained a few parochial schools, but the attendance in the public schools was about ten times as large.

There were three local newspapers in Sandusky— few towns of that size have as many—and in addition to them the people of the county read the Cleveland *Plain Dealer* and a smattering of other out-of-town papers. Of the local papers, one was strongly Republican, one nominally Democratic but actually neutral, and one mildly and belatedly Democratic. The Cleveland *Plain Dealer* broke with its Democratic tradition in 1940 and came out for Willkie. Cleveland and Toledo radio stations covering all the major networks had good reception in Erie County.

The industry of the county was perhaps unusual in that it was scattered among sixty establishments employing about 3000 persons in all and producing a widely diversified array of manufactured items. The largest plant was a paper-box concern employing 900 workers. Sandusky, with a good harbor, was an important port on the Great Lakes, the chief load being coal. Owing partly to the variety of industrial enterprises and partly to widespread dependence upon agriculture, the county had escaped much of the violence of economic shifts during the depression years. The tenor of business affairs was generally conservative and cautious. Because the supply of labor was plentiful, the prevailing wage rate was low. Local union leadership had not been outstanding or progressive or particularly aggressive; the domination of business over labor was freely admitted by local labor leaders. Labor did not form a political bloc as such, and no group or individual was able to deliver the labor vote.

There were no special-interest groups in Erie County wielding important political influence. None of the ethnic groups—Negroes, Germans, or others—formed an organized voting unit. The minority parties were not strong and there was no youth movement in the county (although there was a Young Republican Club). The votes of neither veteran nor fraternal groups could be delivered; and there were too few relief clients for them to be influential as a unit. The 1940 campaign found the Republican party organization tightly knit throughout the county and the Democratic organization split and much less effective.

The major events—local, national, and international —that occurred during the period of the campaign and of the study are represented in Chart 1. They may help to recall the atmosphere of the 1940 campaign.

Social Differences between the Parties

Public opinion research customarily makes use of interviewers' ratings of socioeconomic status, so-called SES ratings. Interviewers are trained to assess the homes, possessions, appearance, and manner of speech of the respondents to classify them into their proper strata in the community according to a set quota. The people with the best homes, furniture, clothes, etc., i.e., the ones with the most money, would be classed as A's; and the people at the other extreme would be D's. These SES ratings are closely related to the educational level of the subjects. Also, the higher ratings go to business and professional people, while the lower ones are given mainly to workers and manual laborers. In short, these ratings represent a sort of average of the status ratings for the different social groups with which people are associated.

Since more than half of the cases in Erie County fell into the C category, these respondents were subclassified on the criterion of telephone ownership. C people with telephones were called C+, those with no telephone C—. Then the quota was approximately in the following distribution: A, 3 per cent; B, 14 per cent; C+, 33 per cent; C—, 30 per cent; and D, 20 per cent.

Now, to what extent did the SES levels differentiate party vote? There were twice as many Republicans on the A level (71 per cent) as on the D level (35 per cent). And with each step down the SES scale the proportion of Republicans decreased and the proportion of Democrats correspondingly increased.

A sociologist interested in the concept of "class" might suggest that it is the objective position of the individual in the system of business and production that matters. For a statistical answer to this problem respondents *within* the different SES levels were subclassified according to their occupations. On each SES level the "upper" occupational groups (professionals, businessmen, clerical and commercial people) were more Republican than the "lower" groups (skilled mechanics, factory workers, and manual laborers).

TABLE 1. 1940 Campaign Events in Erie County

Period	Local Events
May	Interview of poll of 3000
Last half of June	Second interview of panel respondents
First half of July	Third interview of panel, second interview of Control A
Second half of July	
First half of August	Fourth interview of panel, second interview of Control B
Second half of August	Cleveland *Plain Dealer* switches to Willkie
First half of September	
Second half of September	Fifth interview of panel
First half of October	Willkie speaks in Sandusky Last day for vote registration
Second half of October	*Sandusky News* backs Roosevelt Sixth interview of panel, second interview of Control C Gerald L. K. Smith addresses 3000 at Willkie rally in Sandusky
First half of November	Seventh interview of panel

National Events	*International Events*
Knox and Stimson appointed to cabinet	France asks for peace, signs Hitler's terms
GOP votes peace platform; Willkie and McNary nominated	French-Italian armistice signed
Mrs. Roosevelt speaks in Lakeside, Ohio	Churchill announces bulk of French fleet seized or destroyed
Roosevelt says he will not send men overseas	
	Laval announces "corporative" state
Roosevelt and Wallace nominated at Democratic convention	Pan-American Conference in Havana
Debate on conscription	
Lindbergh urges co-operation with Germany if Axis wins	
Roosevelt reiterates: no foreign service for U.S. soldiers	
Willkie makes acceptance speech at Elwood, Indiana	British bomb Berlin in first big raid
Alien registration	
Senate passes draft bill	
FDR calls on the U.S. to unite for total defense	Britain gets U.S. ships in exchange for air and navy bases
Congress passes Draft Act	
	First of 14 days of London air raids
Roosevelt signs Draft Act	German-Italian-Japanese 10-year military alliance
U.S. bans scrap-iron sale to Japan	
Willkie campaign trip through the Middle and Far West	
Roosevelt visits Ohio in "non-political" defense inspection trip	Balkan crisis
Conscription registration	Italy invades Greece
Willkie in the Midwest and East	
Roosevelt's first three campaign speeches	
Last campaign speeches	
Election Day, November 5	

CHART 1. Whereas actual occupation does little to refine the relationship between SES level and vote, it makes more difference whether a voter considers himself as belonging to "business" or "labor."

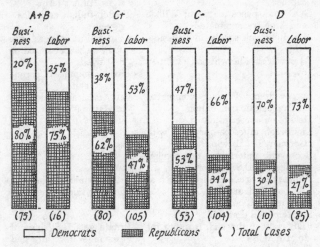

However, once people were classified by the general SES index, the further classification by occupation did not refine the groups very greatly. In other words, people of the same general socioeconomic status have about the same political attitudes regardless of their occupations.

Perhaps a person's own "class" identification influences his vote more than his actual occupation. In order to study this possibility the question was asked, "To which of the following groups do you feel you belong?" For those who did not consider themselves in any of the groups, the following question was raised:

CHART 2. Religious affiliation splits vote sharply. This cannot be attributed to the fact that Catholics in this country are, on the average, lower in SES level than Protestants. The relation between vote and religious affiliation holds true on each SES level.

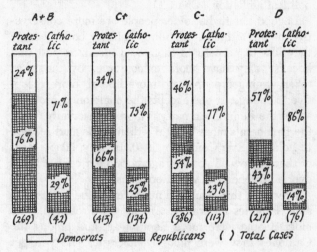

"In which group are you most interested?" The identifications people made in their own minds were more important in determining their votes than their objective occupation (Chart 1). This is not surprising since we here introduced an attitudinal element closely related to factors that influence vote.

In Erie County another factor no less important than SES level was religious affiliation. Sixty per cent of the Protestants and only 23 per cent of the Catholics intended to vote Republican in May. At first glance this might appear to be a spurious result. As a group,

Catholics are ordinarily lower in economic status than Protestants and hence this result may simply have reflected SES levels. But on each SES level religious affiliation played an important role in determining political affiliation (Chart 2).

Legend has it that older people are more conservative in most things, including politics, both because they like to perpetuate their own idealized past and because they have more to conserve. By the same token, younger people are more liberal, more receptive to change. If one accepts the common stereotypes —that the Republican party is more "conservative" and the Democrats more "liberal"—then the legend seemed to hold for Erie County in 1940. In May, 50 per cent of those below 45 years of age but 55 per cent of those over 45 intended to vote Republican.

However, this result did not hold for the Protestants and Catholics separately. Among the Protestants the older people were more Republican, and among the Catholics they were more Democratic. The younger people probably showed less influence of religion upon vote. Thus young Protestants were less Republican than old Protestants and young Catholics less Democratic than old Catholics. The religious factors that influence vote preference are intensified through the years so that they carry more weight for the elderly. They have a longer time to exercise their influence, to indoctrinate the respondent, to affect him through the common elements. In other words, advancing age may not bring *political* conservatism but it does bring *social* conservatism.

A number of other factors were investigated, but

only one proved statistically significant: there were 14 per cent more Republican voters in the rural part of the county than in Sandusky, the one large industrialized town, with a population of 25,000.

In order to use these three factors in a simple way, we constructed an Index of Political Predisposition (IPP) based on SES level, religion, and residence. Of all rich Protestant farmers almost 75 per cent voted Republican, whereas 90 per cent of the Catholic laborers living in Sandusky voted Democratic. Thus respondents could be classified on a scale ranging from those with strong Republican predispositions at one extreme to those with strong Democratic predispositions at the other. While such an index is crude, of course, it did serve to distinguish easily among the votes of people with different combinations of personal characteristics. The proportion of those who voted Republican fell off consistently and significantly from one extreme of political predisposition (74 per cent) to the other (10 per cent). Thus a simple combination of three primary personal characteristics goes a long way in "explaining" political preferences: a person thinks politically as he is socially. Social characteristics determine political preference.

Ideological Differences between the Parties

What the voters believe the victory of their candidate will mean for the country or for themselves should indicate the social philosophy of the two party groups. We therefore asked our panel the following two questions: "What class of people do you think would benefit most by the election of Roosevelt?—by the election of Willkie?"

The pictures of the two candidates as seen through the eyes of the voters was fairly similar for Republicans and Democrats. A very large majority of both groups thought that it would be the common man, the plain people, the working class, who would benefit if Roosevelt were elected. Three quarters of the Democrats explicitly used terms of reference such as "workers" or "laborers," while an equally large majority of the Republicans talked about "WPA jobholders," "relief people," or "unemployed." The two groups, therefore, were agreed on what the social meaning of a Roosevelt victory would be, but his opponents felt that the people Roosevelt would try to help were not the most valuable element of the population.

The two parties did not agree on Willkie as clearly as they did on Roosevelt. While 57 per cent of the Democrats felt that business groups would benefit most from a Willkie victory, only 25 per cent of the Republicans thought so, and 19 per cent of the Republicans claimed that his victory would be beneficial for the working class and the common people.

A second source of data on the social attitudes of the two groups of voters was the arguments people gave to explain their changes in vote intention. More than a third of the Republicans who changed their vote intention from one interview to the next and more than a quarter of the Democrats mentioned economic arguments as reasons. The majority were "class" arguments; one way or another they took a stand on the "poor man—rich man" issue. A "poor man's" argument might be approval of the WPA or a statement that Willkie favored big business or the contention that wages would go down if he were elected. A "rich man's" argument might be that Willkie would restore business confidence or that Roosevelt was ruining business or that he had undermined the self-reliance of the workers by his unemployment policy. The 73 Democrats who cited class arguments usually used "poor man's" arguments exclusively. Of the 49 who switched to Republican, 35 stressed mainly the "rich man's" point of view. The 14 Republicans who explicitly stated that they changed to Willkie because his election would be beneficial to the worker and the common man are an interesting exception. They argued largely in general terms, saying that Willkie would be "for the workingman," or that because he had worked his way up he would understand the needs of the working class.

The arguments can logically be classified in four groups: (1) My candidate is for ——; (2) The other candidate is for ——; (3) The other candidate is against ——; (4) My candidate is against ——. Out of the more than 100 comments we could draw on there was not one case of Type (4): the Democrats never said that Roosevelt was against big business or monopolies, and the Republicans never said Willkie would do away with the WPA or other social legislation. On the other hand, the opposition's candidate was freely accused of being dangerous to specific groups in the population, in arguments of Type (3). The Democrats argued twice as often in favor of Roosevelt's social program as they did against the danger they saw in Willkie's affiliation with big business, while the Republicans pointed to Roosevelt's dangerous economic policies at least as often as they stressed Willkie's value for the businessman.

Our panel was asked: "If you had to choose for President between a man who has had mostly experience in government and a man who has had mostly experience in business, which would you choose?" More than two thirds of the Republicans voted for the businessman, while the same proportion of the Democrats preferred a presidential candidate with government experience. One reason for this difference is that one of the two candidates had come from a business career, and the other one from a career as a public official. To a certain degree, therefore, their followers had to accept this distinction and make the best of it.

But it is hardly a coincidence that the two standard-bearers had such characteristically different pasts. Since the Civil War it has always been the Democratic presidents who symbolized the importance of government as a pursuit of its own. Grover Cleveland was associated with the first success in Civil Service reform. Woodrow Wilson was a professor of government and his notion of the "New Freedom" highlighted the role of government. Roosevelt's New Deal, finally, called for a completely new conception of our governmental institutions. The Republican administrations, on the other hand, were always more concerned with business matters. After the Civil War they were the symbol of expansion toward the West. McKinley had to concentrate on monetary or tariff matters. The three

Republican administrations after World War I were all elected on prosperity platforms, with Harding almost an anti-government candidate. Coolidge thought that "the business of America was business," and Hoover was the "Great Engineer," a representative of successful mining enterprise.

The idea might even be further generalized to the notion of social inclusiveness. We might think of political "extroverts" who take government more seriously than business and who give more weight to international than to national concerns. Thus our respondents were asked: "Do you talk with your friends more about the war or about the coming election?" The Democrats were markedly more interested in the war than the Republicans. They considered private business less important than public affairs, and were relatively more interested in the international scene than in domestic matters.

In the summer of 1940 whether isolationism was possible or desirable was the question of the day. The Republican voters tended more toward the isolationist side and the Democrats less. About 25 per cent of the Republicans opposed both the conscription program and any increase of aid to Britain, whereas only 11 per cent of the Democrats took this "isolationist" position on both questions. The relation was especially clear at the extremes. Of the 38 people who wanted the United States to give less help to England, 82 per cent were Republicans; and of the 42 people who disapproved of the conscription bill even after it was passed, again 82 per cent were Republicans. The Republicans, in almost a solid bloc, stressed keeping

America out of the war. The Democrats were strikingly more likely to see the war situation from the point of view of our possible involvement in it.

This elaboration of the differences between the parties should not be taken to mean that all Democrats disagreed on all issues with all Republicans. In late October, when the formal campaigning reached its most intense stage, each respondent was asked whether he agreed with the following eight arguments then current in the campaign: (1) "Roosevelt has great personal attractiveness, capacity for hard work, and keen intelligence"; (2) "Willkie is a self-made small-town man, who made his way by his genius for industrial organization"; (3) "Willkie is a corporation lawyer whose real sympathies are all with big business"; (4) "The New Deal has interfered too much with private business"; (5) "Roosevelt is rushing the country into war against most of the rest of the world"; (6) "We should not break the democratic tradition by electing any president to a third term"; (7) "With Roosevelt as president, the United States is less likely to yield to Hitler"; and (8) "Willkie will increase production by gaining the confidence of business."

Only 25 per cent of the respondents held the "correct" attitude on all, or nearly all, of eight arguments made by both sides. Similarly, even a week or so after Election Day, 22 per cent of the Republican voters had already bettered their opinion of Roosevelt, now that he had again been elected President. This political tolerance on the part of the voters, both Republicans and Democrats, was more noteworthy in comparison with the partisanship of the campaign managers, although there were a few areas also in campaign argumentation on which the two parties substantially agreed. The two arguments dealing with personality characteristics were the most widely accepted by the respondents. Even Republicans conceded that Roosevelt was intelligent and industrious and even Democrats admitted that Willkie was a success. People apparently prefer to believe that the nominees for the highest office in the land are worthy men, and this factor facilitates the postelection adjustment on the part of those who voted for the loser.

On economic problems the partisans were intent on arguing back and forth, since each side was convinced of the soundness of its own position. However, with another kind of argumentation there was no joining of the issue. There was hardly a Republican who did not mention the third term as a reason for his Republican vote, and there was hardly a Democrat who tried to justify the third term as such. Instead, the Democrats argued against the third term theme by emphasizing the indispensability of Roosevelt's experience in a world at war. And here it was the Republicans who were embarrassed for an answer. They did not argue that such experience was not desirable or necessary, or that Roosevelt really did not have it, or that Willkie did. They simply avoided the issue as such, and tried to compensate for it by stressing the dangers of the third term, experience or not.

Participation in the Election

Some kind of index was necessary to help us classify our respondents according to the extent to which they were psychologically involved in the political events preceding the presidential election. How *interested* were they in the campaign? Among a variety of possible indicators the respondent's self-rating was found to be the best index we had of his interest. It is not surprising that people's self-ratings on interest stood up well under a series of tests of consistency and validity, for being interested is a clearly recognizable experience. The question made sense to almost everyone and almost everyone had a ready answer. People on a higher level of interest (a) had more opinions on issues involved in the election; (b) participated more in election events; and (c) exposed themselves more to the stream of political communications. As the level of interest decreased, (a) the more frequent the "Don't know" answers to certain opinion questions, (b) the lower the index of participation and activity in the campaign, and (c) the less exposure to political communications.

Who were the Interested People? Education and SES level seemed to have about equal importance in creating and maintaining political interest. When both were high, one third of the people expressed great interest in the election; when both were low, this proportion went down to a fifth. In the middle range the two factors approximately compensated one another.

Differences of interest between rural and urban areas were not as great as the stereotype of the isolated farmer might lead one to expect. About 30 per cent of the urban population and 23 per cent of those on farms or in towns of fewer than 2500 population rated themselves on the highest level of interest.

In determining the role of age we had to control the factor of education, for the younger generation has a higher educational level on the average than the older generation. On each educational level the older people were more interested in the election than the younger ones. The prevailing belief that women are less interested in politics than men was corroborated by our data.

The acid test for interest in an election is actual voting. In 1940, Erie County had the high voting record of 81 per cent. This was almost perfectly reflected in our panel, where 82 per cent of the 511 people interviewed after the election reported that they had voted. The greatest proportion of non-voters was indeed found on the lowest interest level. Three-quarters of the non-voters stayed away from the polls deliberately because they were thoroughly unconcerned with the election, and only a small number were kept from the polls by a last-minute emergency. The possibility that the deliberate non-voters could have been made more interested during the campaign is slight; their decision not to vote was too persistent.

The difference in deliberate non-voting between people with more or less education can be completely accounted for by the notion of interest. Deliberate non-voting increases greatly as interest decreases—but if a person is interested, he will vote irrespective of his formal educational level. On the other hand, if he is not interested, he is not likely to vote in any case. A similar picture is obtained for people on different SES levels, for those with different residences, and for different age and religion groups.

Sex differences, alone among the personal characteristics, affected non-voting independently of interest. A man is under more social pressure to go to the polls even if he is not "interested" in the events of the campaign. Not only is it true that these women felt no compulsion to vote, but some of them actually consider their aloofness a virtue: "I have never voted. I never will. . . . A woman's place is in the home. . . . Leave politics to the men." Although legal restrictions upon women's participation in politics were removed some thirty-five years ago, the attitude of women toward politics has not yet brought them to full equality with men.

Time of Final Decision

Interviews with the panel permitted us to distinguish three kinds of voters classified according to the time when they made their *final vote decision*—the decision they followed throughout the rest of the campaign and in the voting booth. Why did some people make up their minds before the campaign began, others not until the end of the campaign? What were the significant differences among these groups?

The more interested people were in the election, the sooner they definitely decided how they would vote. Almost two thirds of the voters with great interest had already made up their minds by May; but considerably less than half of the voters with less interest. Only one eighth of the greatly interested waited until the late period of the campaign before finally deciding how they would vote; twice as many of the less interested delayed their decisions until that period. The campaign managers were thus continuously faced with the task of propagandizing, not only a steadily shrinking segment of the electorate, but also a segment whose interest in and concern with the election also steadily shrank. By the end of the campaign the managers were exerting their greatest efforts to catch a few votes of the least interested persons.

A vote decision can be considered the net effect of a variety of pressures. Now what if these individual factors work in opposite directions? Suppose an individual is *both* prosperous and Catholic? How will he make up his mind? Or suppose he belongs to the Protestant faith and lives in a poor section of the community? Which of the conflicting influences will win out? People who are subject to contradictory and opposing influences of this kind are said to be under cross-pressures. The more evenly balanced these opposing pressures were, the longer the voter delayed in making up his mind.

We used six instances of cross-pressure to show their effect in delaying the time of decision.

1. *Religion and SES Level:* Protestants on lower SES levels (C— and D) and Catholics on upper SES levels (A, B, and C+) were subject to this cross-pressure.

2. *Occupation and Identification:* Some semi-skilled and unskilled workers tended to think of themselves as belonging with the business class, and a few white-collar people thought of themselves as belonging with labor. Since the business group ordinarily supported one party and the labor group the other, a cross-pressure was set up between the voter's objective occupation and his subjective identification.

3. *1936 Vote and 1940 Vote:* The voters who changed between the 1936 and the 1940 elections—primarily made up of persons who had voted for Roosevelt in 1936 but were for Willkie in 1940—could be regarded as having something of a tradition to overcome.

4. *The Voter and His Family:* Sometimes other members of the respondent's family disagreed with him and oftener other members of the family were undecided. In either case the respondent was under a cross-pressure between the views of two members of the family or between his own ideas and those of at least one other member of his family. Of the six cross-pressures this was the most effective one in delaying vote decision.

5. *The Voter and His Associates:* Friends as well as family created a political environment. Respondents who noticed trends toward the opposition party were subjected thereby to conflicting pressures from their associates.

6. *1940 Vote Intention and Attitude toward Business and Government:* Some Republicans wanted government experience in their presidential candidate, and some Democrats thought business experience was more important. These deviates were subject to a certain amount of cross-pressure.

Whatever the source of the conflicting pressures, the result was to delay the voter's final decision. As shown (in Chart 3), the voters who were subject to cross-pressures on their vote decided later than the voters for whom the various factors reinforced one another.

Simply because they had good reasons for voting for both candidates it was difficult for people subject to

CHART 3. People who are exposed to cross-pressures delay their final vote decision. This chart represents those with great interest, but the same relation holds for those with less interest.

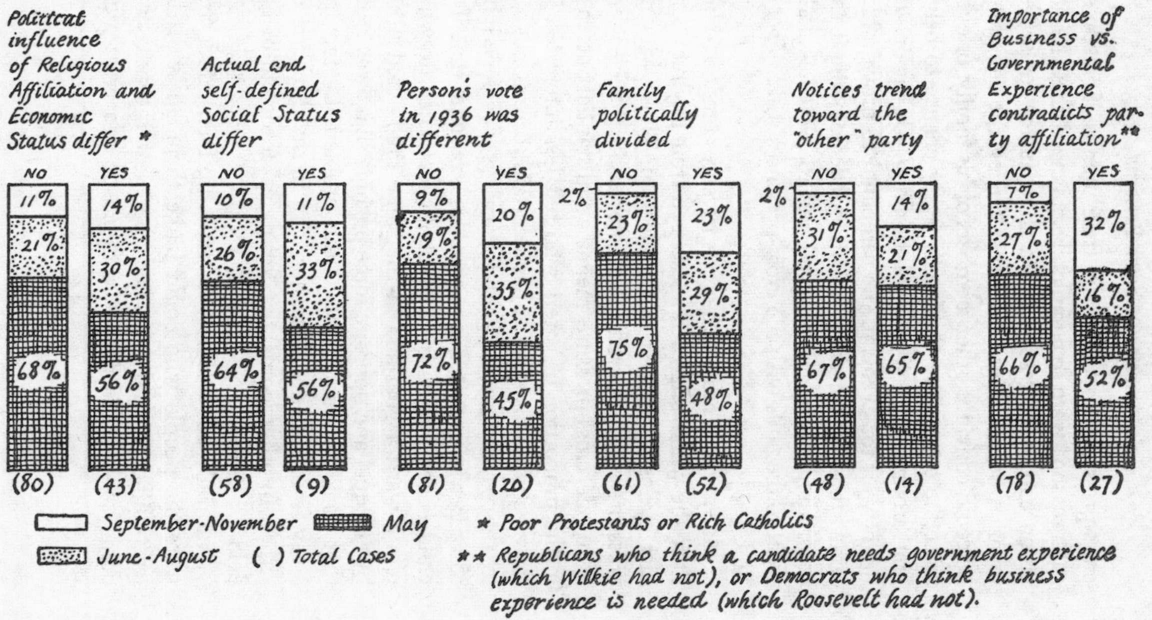

Political Influence of Religious Affiliation and Economic Status differ *

NO (80): 11% / 21% / 68%
YES (43): 14% / 30% / 56%

Actual and self-defined Social Status differ

NO (58): 10% / 26% / 64%
YES (9): 11% / 33% / 56%

Person's vote in 1936 was different

NO (81): 9% / 19% / 72%
YES (20): 20% / 35% / 45%

Family politically divided

NO (61): 2% / 23% / 75%
YES (52): 23% / 29% / 49%

Notices trend toward the "other" party

NO (48): 2% / 31% / 67%
YES (14): 14% / 21% / 65%

Importance of Business vs. Governmental Experience contradicts party affiliation **

NO (78): 7% / 27% / 66%
YES (27): 32% / 16% / 52%

September-November ▢   May ▨   Juno-August ▨   ( ) Total Cases

* Poor Protestants or Rich Catholics

** Republicans who think a candidate needs government experience (which Willkie had not), or Democrats who think business experience is needed (which Roosevelt had not).

cross-pressures to make up their minds. Sometimes such reasons were so completely balanced that the decision had to be referred to a third factor for settlement. A person might hope that during the campaign he could convince other members of his family, or even more, he might give the family every chance to bring him around to their way of thinking. Or, again, he might wait for events in the campaign to provide him with a basis for making up his mind. Sometimes the contradiction was not resolved and the voter actually went to the polls with the cross-pressures still in operation.

Many voters subject to cross-pressures tended to belittle the whole affair: they escaped from any real conflict by losing interest in the election. Those with no cross-pressures showed most interest in the election; even one cross-pressure meant a substantial increase in the proportion of voters who felt less interested in the election. This relation has a certain correspondence to the psychological "field theory" as developed by Kurt Lewin. Lewin has shown, for example, that if a child is acted upon by a psychological force drawing him toward a goal and at the same time acted upon by an equal and opposite force pushing him away from that goal, he would "solve" the problem by moving away from both forces rather than in the direction of either. In other words, the "resultant" leads out of the field.

Naturally, the people who made up their minds first were the people who *could* make them up with the least difficulty and who had the most incentive for doing so—i.e., the people with no or one cross-pressure in voting background and with great interest in the election. Fully three fourths of them knew in May how they would vote in November, while only 7 per cent of them waited until the last weeks of the campaign before settling their vote intentions once and for all. At the other extreme were the people subject to two or more cross-pressures and without much interest in the election. Only one fourth of them made a final decision as early as May and fully one third waited until the last period of the campaign before finally making up their minds.

The comparison between cross-pressures and lack of interest is not fully expressed in these quantitative statements. If the voter faces a clear-cut situation, free from cross-pressures, then interest determines how soon his practically inevitable decision will be precipitated. Awareness of the election is paralleled at once by recognition of his "natural" position. If the voter happens to be faced by cross-pressures, then interest operates a little differently. Where interest is not too strong, the tendency is to dismiss the whole issue as not making very much difference. The line of least resistance is not to vote at all, and many such people do not vote. Strong interest may overcome the impulse to avoid the matter and keep the prospective but puzzled voter arguing the case with himself and his friends until Election Day forces a decision or some incident serves to swing the close balance of decision. Great interest tends to bring a decision *as such,* whereas lack of conflicting pressures brings a decision *for* one or the other party.

The panel was interviewed for the sixth time during

October and for the seventh and final time immediately after the election. Thus we know how these people intended to vote shortly before the election and for whom they actually voted. The results were as in Table 2. This simple table has a surprising number of impli-

TABLE 2. Vote Intention in October Compared with Actual Vote in November

| | Vote Intention in October | | | | |
Actual Vote	Repub-lican	Demo-crat	Don't Know	Don't Expect to Vote	Total
Republican	215	7	4	6	232
Democrat	4	144	12	0	160
Didn't vote	10	16	6	59	91
Total	229	167	22	65	483

cations. Let us assume for a moment that the interviews in October and November had been conducted with a different sample of the population each time rather than always with the same panel. Then the findings would have read as follows: in October, 42 per cent (167 out of 396) of those who had a vote intention meant to vote for the Democratic party; in November 41 per cent (160 out of 392) voted for it. This would have given the impression of great constancy in political attitudes. Actually, however, only the people in the major diagonal of the table (indicated by bold type) remained unchanged: 418 out of 483 respondents did what they intended to do; 13 per cent changed their minds one way or another. This 13 per cent represents the *turnover* that took place in the few weeks before the election, and this concept of turnover is basic for analysis of opinion formation. If the turnover is large, it indicates that the opinion or behavior is unstable. We know that people feel uncertain and that propaganda may be effective, or that clarification and education are required.

The Types of Changes

The people who did not make up their minds until some time during the campaign proper differed in the ways in which they came to their final vote decision. In this sense the three main kinds of changers were the following (the figures are percentages of the voters as a whole):

28 per cent Crystallizers: They are people who had no vote intention in May but later acquired one; they went from "Don't know" to Republican (14 per cent) or from "Don't know" to Democrat (14 per cent).

15 per cent Waverers: They are people who started out with a vote intention, then fell away from it—either to "Don't know" (11 per cent) or to the other party (4 per cent)—and later returned to their original choice.

8 per cent Party Changers: They are people who started out with a vote intention and later changed to the other party, finally voting for it. They went from Republican to Democrat (2 per cent) or from Democrat to Republican (6 per cent).

The three kinds of changers—the crystallizers, the waverers, and the party changers—all came to their final decision some time after May, but not all at the same time. The crystallizers decided much earlier than the others. There were those who wavered only to indecision and there were those who wavered all the way to the other party, and this "distance" of the wavering was significant for time of final decision. The people who intended at times during the campaign to vote for both parties took much longer to reach a final vote decision than those who varied only between one of the parties and indecision.

The more interest and the fewer conflicting pressures a person had, the more he tended to decide, not only early in the campaign, but also definitely—and never to change his mind thereafter (Chart 4). If a person had somewhat less interest and somewhat more cross-pressures, then he tended to doubt longer and oftener than the constants, but he slid back only to a tentative "Don't know." Only those people who had much less interest and many more conflicting pressures vacillated between the two parties.

The two-party changers were the people who were torn in both directions and did not have enough interest in the election to cut through the conflicting pressures upon them and come to a deliberate and definite decision. They drifted. These people, the only ones of the entire electorate to make a complete change during the campaign were: the least interested in the election; the least concerned about its outcome; the least attentive to political material in the formal media of communication; the last to settle upon a vote decision; and the most likely to be persuaded, finally, by a personal contact, not an "issue" of the election. The notion that the people who switch parties during the campaign are mainly the reasoned, thoughtful, con-

CHART 4. The less interest people have and the more cross-pressures to which they are subject, the more variable are their vote intentions.

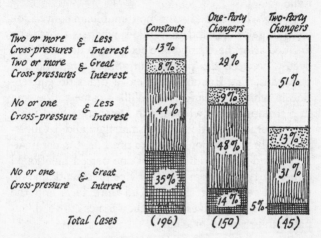

scientious people who were convinced by the issues of the election is just plain wrong.

Constants were reported to be more self-assured, better informed, more co-operative, and broader in their interests. All the traits corresponded to their greater enthusiasm for the political campaign. Voters who had changed their vote intentions previously were three times as likely to change on the next interview as those who had.

What were the social factors that influenced the voters' decisions? The first influence upon the changers as a whole came in June, with the fall of France. Of the people who definitely decided their vote in June two thirds decided for the Democrats, mainly on the ground that the European crisis necessitated the continuance of an experienced administration in Washington.

Voters who decided after the Republican convention were largely attracted to Willkie, whereas those who decided after the Democratic convention divided more evenly between the parties but still favored the Republicans. The Republicans held a dramatic convention in which the dark horse Willkie came to the fore in a striking finish, whereas the Democrats held what was generally regarded as a mismanaged and flat meeting that broke a major American precedent in nominating a third-term candidate. Not one person mentioned either party's platform or either vice-presidential nominee as a reason for change. The third term and the candidates themselves were the "issues" that dominated the reasons for change.

The Activation Effect

Knowing a few of the respondents' personal characteristics, we could tell with fair certainty how they would finally vote: they would join the fold to which they belonged. We recall that if a person was Catholic, lived within the city of Sandusky, and belonged in the lower half of the SES scale, there was a strong likelihood that he would vote Democratic. Similarly, those with the strongest Republican predispositions were prosperous Protestant farmers. Thus about two thirds of the crystallizers with a Republican predisposition decided by October to vote Republican, and about three fourths of those with a Democratic predisposition decided for the Democrats. From a simple three-factor index we could predict with considerable accuracy the outcome of deliberations that the deciders themselves could not foresee. What the political campaign did in these cases was not to form new opinions but to raise old opinions over the thresholds of awareness and decision. Political campaigns are important primarily because they *activate* latent predispositions.

The activating forces of political communications are, first, materials in the formal mass media—the newspaper, magazine, and radio; secondly, direct personal influences.

There are four continuous steps in the normal process of activation: (1) Propaganda arouses interest; (2) Increased interest brings increased exposure; (3) Attention is selective; (4) Votes crystallize. It was possible to study closely the relation between exposure to propaganda and the level of interest. It was not the passage of time alone that accounted for the increase in interest, nor differences in initial level of interest, but the greater exposure to campaign propaganda.

The voter who lives in the country reads farm journals that happen also to be more Republican; or he lives in the city and so hears more talk from fellow-workers who are pro-labor and pro-Democratic. The environment sifts the propaganda that the respondent sees and hears. Moreover, while most people read newspapers for the daily news, the sports pages, the comics, etc.—material that is the same in most newspapers—a Republican will prefer to get it from a Republican newspaper as a sort of symbol that he belongs to his own political group. In times of a presidential campaign, when the newspapers start to take definite views on current events, the two groups then find themselves more and more exposed to the arguments of their own side.

People selected political material in accord with their own taste and bias, including even those who had not yet made a decision. The people who in August did not have a definite vote intention were classified into those with social characteristics that should have predisposed them to be Democrats and Republicans. All the speeches, magazine articles, or newspaper stories they reported reading or hearing were classified according to their political content. The still undecided persons with the economic, religious, and residential attributes that usually characterize Republicans managed as a rule to see and hear more Republican propaganda; and similarly for those predisposed to be Democrats. From his many past experiences shared with others in his economic, religious, and community groups the voter has a readiness to attend to some things more than others. It is likely that a desire for reinforcement of one's own point of view exists, and it is probably a pleasant experience to read something with which one is familiar if the stage of boredom has not yet been reached.[1] In times of politi-

[1] Such partisan exposure is not confined to politics. For example, educational broadcasts reach primarily those people who need them least: in a recent series of programs on the contributions of various national minorities to American life, the audience for each program was primarily composed of the members of the particular minority group being extolled. People even tend to read advertisements of the things they already own and listen to the radio programs sponsored by the company that manufactures their most important possessions.

cal crisis there seems to be a tendency to listen endlessly to commentators who tell the same story with minor variations.

Political writers have the task of providing "rational" man with good and acceptable reasons to dress up the choice that is more effectively determined by underlying social affiliations. Arguments enter the final stage of decision more as *indicators* than as *influences*. They *point out*, like signboards along the road, the way to turn in order to reach a destination that is already determined. The political predisposition and group allegiances set the goal; all that is read and heard becomes helpful and effective in so far as it guides the voter toward his already "chosen" destination. The clinching argument thus does not have the function of *persuading* the voter to act. He furnishes the motive power himself. The argument has the function of *identifying* for him the way of thinking and acting that he is already half aware of wanting.

A campaign argument will be particularly successful if a variety of meanings can be read into it. One of the slogans in favor of Willkie, for example, was that he represented the American ideal of the poor boy who made good. From this picture of the man who started humbly and became successful any one of three different elements may be brought to the fore: the poor people can feel that he will not have forgotten them, the rich people can be convinced that he will take care of their interests, and the middle-class voters can be attracted by the implications of hard work and thrift, which are so prominent in their own ideology. Structured stereotypes are too well defined to be useful. The unstructured are catchalls into which each voter reads the meanings he desires.

The Reinforcement Effect

Half the people in our study knew in May, before the campaign got under way, how they would vote in November, and actually voted that way. For them political communications served the important purpose of preserving prior decisions instead of initiating new ones. Campaign propaganda had the effect of reinforcing the original vote decision.

A continuous flow of partisan arguments enables the voter to reinterpret otherwise unsettling events and counterarguments so that they do not leave him in an uncomfortable state of mental indecision or inconsistency. For example, Republicans who might be disturbed by Willkie's relation to utility interests were equipped with the notion that his experience in business would make him a better administrator of the national government than Roosevelt. Similarly, Democrats uneasy about the third term as a break with American tradition were able to justify it by reference to the President's indispensable experience in foreign affairs during such a world crisis.

In Erie County in 1940 there was much more Republican material available, but it was still reasonably easy to read or listen to the Democratic side. The universe of campaign communications—political speeches, newspaper stories, newscasts, editorials, columns, magazine articles—was open to virtually everyone. But since exposure was consistently partisan, it resulted in reinforcement. The more strongly partisan the person, the more likely he was to insulate himself from contrary points of view. The constants with great interest and with most concern in the election of their own candidate were *more* partisan in exposure than the constants with less interest and less concern. In short, the most partisan people protect themselves from the disturbing experience presented by opposition arguments by paying little attention to them. Instead, they turn to the propaganda that reaffirms the validity and wisdom of their original decision, which is then reinforced.

One of the assumptions of a two-party democratic system is that considerable intercommunication goes on between the supporters of the opposing sides. In recent years there has been a good deal of talk by men of good will about the desirability and necessity of guaranteeing the free exchange of ideas in the market place of public opinion. Such talk has centered upon the problem of keeping free the channels of expression and communication. But the consumers of ideas themselves erect high tariff walls against alien notions.

The influence exerted upon the waverers by the media of communication to return to their original decisions was no less a reinforcement effect than that exerted upon someone who doubted but never actually left his party. It is just that they needed *more* reinforcement.

Consider the case of a young unemployed laborer on a low SES level—a "natural" Democrat. Originally Democratic, he decided in August to vote Republican because of the third-term issue. But then he heard an argument that served to reinforce his Democratic predispositions: "I heard a Lowell Thomas broadcast yesterday saying that *Hitler and Mussolini wanted Willkie elected.*" Another illustration, the vice-president of a bank, with strong Republican predispositions, was Republican in May, but by June—after Germany's conquest of Western Europe—he was not sure: "My decision will depend upon who will keep us out of war. That is paramount in my mind." But all his attitudes and values, and probably associates, were so firmly Republican that his indecision was short-lived. "I've read articles about Willkie in the Cleveland *Plain Dealer* and also the Chicago *Tribune.* I have also read a book, *The Smoke Screen*, which woke me up to just how badly FDR is spending the taxpayers' money."

When people speak of the influence of the press and radio, usually they mean conversion. Some people were converted by campaign propaganda, but they were few indeed. The people who did most of the reading and listening not only read and heard most of their own partisan propaganda but were also most resistant to conversion because of their strong predispositions. And the people who were most open to conversion—the ones the campaign managers most wanted to reach—read and listened least. Those interrelated facts represent the bottleneck of conversion.

Nevertheless exposure to partisan propaganda did lead some people to vote against their predispositions. A certain proportion exposed to propaganda in opposition to their predisposition voted in line with the propaganda and out of line with their predisposition.

In 1940 the major Republican argument—perhaps the major issue of the whole campaign—was the third term. What success did it have in converting people? Let us say that the third-term issue *could have* converted to a 1940 Republican vote only those who (1) voted for Roosevelt in 1936 *and* (2) did not intend in May 1940 to vote Republican (i.e., before Roosevelt was nominated) *and* (3) believed that Roosevelt had been a good president. Only fifteen persons who voted Republican qualified on all three criteria of Democratic sympathy. Of those only nine gave the third term as the most important reason for their final vote decision, and only six as the *sole* reason. The third-term issue served as a "real" converting influence only for these few people—about 2 per cent of the total Republican vote. And even then, probably not all six were "real" converts, since five of them, who had mixed political predispositions tending toward Republican, were partly activated and only partly converted to a Republican vote. The one clear case of the effectiveness of the third-term argument was a poor Catholic carpenter on the lowest SES level, obviously a man with strong Democratic predispositions. He had voted for Roosevelt in 1932 and 1936 (and for Al Smith in 1928), he approved what Roosevelt had accomplished, and he originally had planned to vote for him again—but "the third term is a stumbling block." In August he finally decided to vote Republican.

Thus, in so far as mass media of communications led to conversion at all, it was through a redefinition of the issues. In this example and others, issues about which people had previously thought very little or had been little concerned took on a new importance as they were accented by campaign propaganda. In this way political communications occasionally broke down traditional party loyalties.

Only a very small number of respondents who were greatly interested in the election felt that there was something important to be said for each side, and tried more or less conscientiously to resolve their doubts one way or the other during the campaign. They, and only they, conformed to the standard stereotype of the dispassionate, rational democratic voter. For the most part such persons had "weak" predispositions, i.e., they tended to fall at or near the center of the IPP score. In other words, their social position was such that they could "afford" conversion through thought. The real doubters—the open-minded voters who make a sincere attempt to weigh the issues and the candidates dispassionately in terms of the good of the country as a whole—exist mainly in deferential campaign propaganda, in textbooks on civics, in the movies, and in the minds of some political idealists.

The Band-Wagon Effect

The influence of expectation on vote intention is psychologically a rather complicated one. Probably some people had already half made up their minds for whom to vote, but it seemed less dangerous to put it in the form of an expectation rather than vote intention. In other cases hearing about a candidate's chances might have activated a predisposition already existing. But in some cases respondents did not hesitate to say straight out that they were deliberately trying to vote for the winner.

At every interview we asked our respondents the following question: "Regardless of which man or party you would like to see elected, which party do you think actually will be elected?" Although the respondents were Republican in the majority, more expected the Democrats to win. By and large, however, each party expected its own candidate to win, and the people who had no vote intention were also not interested enough to form much of an opinion as to the probable winner. The greater the interest in the election, the closer was the relation between expectation and vote intention.

When people explained their changes in vote *intention*, they gave as sources of their decision radio or newspaper or personal conversations with other people in about the same frequency. But when they named their reasons for change in *expectation*, they mentioned face-to-face contacts with other people slightly more frequently than both formal media taken together.

There seemed to be two main ways in which people influenced each other's expectations. First, someone was told by someone else that the chances of a candidate had changed, as exemplified in the following quotation from an interview: "*People say* each time Willkie speaks he loses a lot of votes. I don't know myself but I believe he may lose out."

Secondly, the respondent formed his own conclusions by watching what went on around him. He did not need to be told because he could see the signs on the wall himself: "On previous interviews it seemed as though more people were for Roosevelt. But the third term is against him, *the people don't like* the way he made the trade with England for the naval bases without conferring with Congress, so now I am not so sure any more who will win."

It is interesting to observe that as the campaign progressed the former kind of remark decreased and the latter kind of comment increased, until in October the two kinds of comments were about equally frequent.

The campaign itself, however, reshuffled the respondents' environment so that, politically, it became more consistent with their own views. Each of the two main political environments operated as a kind of magnetic force. The changes taking place around Republican observers were, in a majority of the cases, in a Republican direction. And, conversely, wherever changes in favor of Roosevelt were noticed, they were reported by Democratic observers. This result cannot be entirely explained by the mechanism of projection, for the Democratic as well as the Republican respondents observed more changes in favor of Willkie. And this indicates the realistic nature of our respondents' observations, for it is known that the county became more and more Republican as the campaign progressed.

The Over-All Effect of the Campaign

The proper perspective on a presidential campaign is gained only by a consideration of the changes from one presidential election to another. Only then can one basic question be answered: Does the formal campaign during the summer and fall of an election year simply extend the long-term voting trend evident from election to election? Or does the campaign hasten or retard the trend line? In other words, what does the campaign do that would not have been done by the mere passage of time? From a low of 35 per cent of the two-party vote in 1924, the Democrats reached a peak of 62 per cent in 1936. Between 1936 and 1940 the Democratic majority fell off, but remained a majority. How much of such gross change occurs *between* one election and the beginning of the next campaign and how much occurs *during* the campaign?

In Erie County in 1940 changes in vote intention during the campaign were many fewer than during the preceding three and a half years. All the events of the intermediate period—local, national, and international —changed over twice as many votes as all the events of the campaign. What the campaign did was to speed up the long-term trend toward the Republicans. The movement away from the Democrats from 1936 to 1940 was activated, so to speak, by the campaign.

The presidential campaign as a whole—the speeches, the events, the writings, the discussions, the total propaganda output—had three effects upon the voters. The campaign activated the indifferent, reinforced the partisan, and converted the doubtful. The three effects are summarized in Table 3, which covers all the possible vote combinations as of May and October, from the beginning to the end of the campaign. The figure for activation is probably low and the figure for conversion is probably high. In any case conversion is, by far, the least frequent result and activation the second most frequent manifest effect of the campaign.

TABLE 3. The Effect of the Campaign upon Vote Intentions (May and October)

Vote Intention in May	Vote Intention in October			
	Followed Predisposition	Ran Counter to Predisposition	Was Undecided	Total
Followed Predisposition	Reinforcement 36%	Conversion 2%	Partial Conversion 3%	41%
Ran Counter to Predisposition	Reconversion 3%	Reinforcement 17%	Partial Conversion 3%	23%
Was Undecided	Activation 14%	Conversion 6%	No effect 16%	36%
Total	53%	25%	22%	100%

The Political Homogeneity of Social Groups

Voting is essentially a group experience. People who work or live or play together are likely to vote for the same candidates. People who have certain characteristics in common—for example, age—are most likely to belong to the same groups. Each of the three factors on which our Index of Political Predisposition was based—SES level, religious affiliation, and residence—plays an important role in deciding what type of people will have close personal contact with each other. People who have similar IPP ratings are likely to live in closer contact with each other, and the groups they form are likely to be rather homogeneous in political outlook and behavior. This tendency is accentuated during the course of the campaign, for changes in vote intention increase group homogeneity.

The family is a group particularly suited to the purposes of our study, because here living conditions attain a maximum of similarity and because mutual contacts are more frequent than in other groups. Only 4 per cent of the 413 panel members who voted said that someone in their families had voted differently from themselves. The extent of disagreement increased slightly toward the end of the campaign, which is consistent with the finding that people under crosspressure make their final vote intention late.

Among husbands and wives, both of whom had decided to vote, only one pair in twenty-two disagreed. The almost perfect agreement came about as a result of male dominance in political situations. When we asked each respondent whether he or she had discussed politics with someone else in recent weeks, forty-five of the women stated that they had talked the election over with their husbands; but, of an equal number of randomly selected men, only four reported discussions with their wives. Men did not feel that they are discussing politics with their wives; they felt they were telling them.

The level of interest was contagious from one family member to another. Of the men who had a vote intention and great interest in the election only 30 per cent said that their wives did not intend to vote, or did not know for whom. For men with less interest the comparable figure was 52 per cent.

Two *first voters* took over the family pattern at the very beginning of their voting careers: "I probably will vote Democratic because *my grandfather will skin me if I don't.*" "If I can register I will vote Republican because *my family are all Republicans, so therefore I would have to vote that way.*" Neither had much interest in the election and neither paid much attention to the campaign. Both accepted family tradition for their first votes and both are likely to remain in line with that tradition.

Political conformity is often the price of domestic peace. There was evidence of a good deal of tension in families that could not reach an agreement. One girl reported in June that she intended to vote for the Democratic party, because she "liked the Democratic candidates better than the Republicans." She finally broke down and voted for Willkie, explaining, "*My father and friends* thought it would be a good idea not to have Roosevelt for a third term, because he would be too much of a dictator."

Whatever the reason for changes in vote intention, whether honest conviction or family loyalty, the family molded votes—and as a result the family became politically more homogeneous as the campaign wore on.

Our sample was too small to study specific organizations, but we could distinguish between those people who belonged to formal organizations and those who did not. In general, members of any given organization were recruited from fairly similar socioeconomic levels. Secondly, people on the lower SES levels were less likely to belong to any organizations than the people on high SES levels. Although the proportion of Republicans was generally large on high SES levels, the Republican trend was still stronger among those who had joined various associations. Simply meeting more often with other persons, even in organizations not ostensibly concerned with politics, probably activated predispositions more. Similarly, in his union the worker of C— or D economic level associated with, and was stimulated by, others of a like predisposition. As a result, on the C— and D levels, only 31 per cent of those who were union members but 53 per cent of those who were not union members voted Republican.

One final observation demonstrates that during the campaign social groups imbue their individual members with the accepted political ideology of the group. In August there were, for instance, thirty-three Republicans who felt that government experience is more important in a president, and thirty Democrats who thought that business experience would be more desirable. Of those who harmonized this inconsistent attitude pattern by October almost all retained their party allegiance. This was true for whatever specific opinion we took. If a person's vote intention is to a great degree a symbol of the social group to which he or she belongs, then we should not be surprised that people iron out inconsistencies in their thinking in such a way as to conform to the group with which they live from day to day. In a way people vote, not only *with* their social group, but also *for* it.

In short, social groups are politically homogeneous and the campaign increases this homogeneity still more. People who live together under similar external conditions are likely to develop similar needs and interests. They tend to apply to common experiences common interpretations. They will approve of a political candidate who has achieved success in their own walk of life; they will approve of programs couched in terms taken from their own occupations and adapted to the moral standards of the groups in which they have a common "belonging." But there may be many group members who are not really aware of the goals of their own group or, even if aware, not sufficiently interested in current events to tie the two together consciously. They acquiesce to the political temper of their group under the steady, personal influence of their more politically active fellow citizens.

The Nature of Personal Influence

Common observation and many community studies show that in every area and for every public issue there are certain people who are most concerned about the issue as well as most articulate about it. We call them

The People's Choice

the "opinion leaders." At about the middle of the campaign the panel respondents were asked these two questions: "Have you tried to convince anyone of your political ideas recently?" "Has anyone asked your advice on a political question recently?" All those who answered "Yes" to either or both of these questions— 21 per cent of the panel group—were designated as opinion leaders. Their responses to other questions during the series of interviews, as well as subsequent checkups on their objective roles within certain groups, established the validity of the identification.

Opinion leaders are not identical with the socially prominent people in the community or the richest people or the civic leaders. They are found in all occupational groups (Table 4). In all respects the opinion leaders demonstrated greater political alertness. On each level of interest the opinion leaders read more

TABLE 4. Proportion of Opinion Leaders in Various Occupations

Occupation	Total Number of Persons	Opinion Leaders
Professional	17	35%
Proprietary, managerial	28	25
Clerical	21	33
Commercial, sales	16	44
Skilled workers	37	35
Semi-skilled workers	31	32
Unskilled workers	47	23
Farmers	46	15
Housewives	230	13
Unemployed	13	15
Retired	23	35

and listened more to campaign material; they talked politics more than the others.

Whenever the respondents were asked to report on their recent exposure to campaign communications of all kinds, political discussions were mentioned more frequently than exposure to radio or print. But opinion leaders reported that the formal media were more effective as sources of influence than personal relations. This suggests that ideas often flow from radio and print to the opinion leaders and from them to the less active sections of the population.

The weight of personal contacts upon opinion lies, paradoxically, in their greater casualness. If we read or tune in a speech, we usually have a definite mental set that tinges our receptiveness. Such purposive behavior is part of the broad area of our political experiences, to which we bring our convictions with a desire to test them and strengthen them by what is said. This mental set is armor against influence. On the other hand, people we meet for reasons other than political discussion are more likely to catch us unprepared, so to speak, if they make politics the topic. Politics gets through, especially to the indifferent, much more easily by personal contacts than in any other way, simply because it comes up unexpectedly as a side-line or marginal topic in a casual conversation. Overheard bits of conversation are particularly effective, for since one need not be suspicious as to the persuasive intentions of the speakers, one's defenses are down. Furthermore, one may feel that one is getting the viewpoint of "people generally," that one is learning how "different people" think about the election: "I've heard fellows talk at the plant . . . I hear men talk at the shop . . . My husband heard that talked about at work . . ."

When someone yields to a personal influence in making a vote decision, the reward is immediate and personal. A neighbor can "punish" one immediately for being unimpressed or unyielding to a political argument: he can look angry or sad, he can leave the room and make his fellow feel isolated. A pamphlet can only intimate or describe future deprivations; the living person can create them at once.

Personal contact has another advantage compared with other media: the face-to-face contact can counter resistance, for it is much more flexible. In propaganda as much as in other things, one man's meat is another man's poison. The formal media produced several boomerangs upon people who resented what they read or heard and moved in the opposite direction from that intended. But among fifty-eight respondents who mentioned personal contacts as concretely influential there was only one boomerang.

The doubtful voter may feel that the evaluations he reads or hears in a broadcast are plausible, but he still wonders whether these are the issues that are really going to affect *his own* future welfare. But he can trust the judgment and evaluation of the respected people among his asasociates, most of whom are people with the same status and interests as himself. Their attitudes are more relevant for him than the judgments of an unknown editorial writer. In a formal communication the content can be at its best; but in a face-to-face contact the transference is most readily achieved.

Trust in another person's point of view may be caused by his prestige as well as by the plausibility of what he has to say or its relevancy to one's interests. The driver of a bread truck changed to Willkie because the prominent president of a business firm had done him the honor of persuading him in that direction. A middle-aged housewife with little education shifted from Willkie because of the statements of people she considered authorities: "I talked with *a college student* from Case, in Cleveland, and students are for Roosevelt because he has helped recreation."

Finally, personal contacts can get a voter to the polls without affecting at all his comprehension of the issues of the election—something the formal media can rarely do. The newspaper or magazine or radio must first be effective in changing attitudes related to the action. There were several clear cases of votes cast not on the issues or even the personalities of the candidates. In fact, they were not really cast for the candidates at all but for the voters' friends.

One should not identify the personal contacts discussed here with the efforts of the professional political machines. These personal contacts are what one might call amateur machines that spring up during elections —individuals who become quite enthusiastic or special groups that try to activate people within their reach. One might almost say that the most successful form of propaganda—especially last-minute propaganda—is to "surround" the people whose vote decision is still dubious, so that the only path left to them is the way to the polling booth.

In the last analysis, more than anything else, people

can move other people. From an ethical point of view this is a hopeful aspect in propaganda, for the side that has the more enthusiastic supporters and that can mobilize grass-root support in an expert way has great chances of success.

Suggestions for Further Reading

MORRIS JANOWITZ AND WARREN E. MILLER. "The Index of Political Predisposition in the 1948 Election," *Journal of Politics*, 14:4 (November 1952), 710–27. A test of the IPP against national data indicated that it needed refinement. It seemed to predict the conservative vote better than the protest vote.

BERNARD R. BERELSON, PAUL F. LAZARSFELD, AND WILLIAM N. MCPHEE. *Voting: A Study of Opinion Formation in a Presidential Campaign* (Chicago: University of Chicago Press, 1954). A study similar to that reported in *The People's Choice*, based on a survey in Elmira, New York.

ANGUS CAMPBELL *et al. The Voter Decides* (Evanston, Illinois: Row, Peterson, 1954). "A study of the voter's perceptions, attitudes, and behaviors, based on a survey of the 1952 election." The emphasis is on psychological rather than social determinants of political preferences.

FREDERICK MOSTELLER *et al. The Pre-Election Polls of 1948* (New York: Social Science Research Council, 1949). A critical analysis of why the public-opinion polls in 1948 generally predicted the election of Dewey rather than Truman. Chapter 9 on "Political Behavior and Voting" is particularly relevant.

LOUIS H. BEAN. *How to Predict Elections* (New York: Knopf, 1948). A better book than its title would indicate.

Contrary to the general trend of expert opinion, Bean correctly predicted the election of Truman in 1948.

SAMUEL LUBELL. *The Future of American Politics* (New York: Harper, 1951). Combines the analysis of national trends of Bean with an approach to the intensive local studies exemplified by *The People's Choice*. A stimulating and original work presented in a popular style.

V. O. KEY, JR. *Southern Politics in State and Nation* (New York: Knopf, 1949). In a different tradition from *The People's Choice,* but as much of a pioneer work in political analysis.

Union Democracy and Secondary Organization*

SEYMOUR MARTIN LIPSET, MARTIN A. TROW,
& JAMES S. COLEMAN

In recent years political democracy has proved so
vulnerable to variations in social structure that the
better understanding of the social processes that support democracy has become one of the major tasks
of social science. Few still believe (as the American

*This study of the political system of the ITU was conducted
for the Bureau of Applied Social Research of Columbia University. The research was supported by grants from the Rocke-
feller Foundation, the American Philosophical Society, the Council on Research in the Social Sciences of Columbia University,
and the Publications Fund of the Bureau of Applied Social
Research.

This essay is an integrated summary of one section of *Union
Democracy* (Glencoe, Ill.: Free Press, 1956), by the authors.
Specifically it contains matter presented in Chapters I, IV, and
V of the larger study. The reader is cautioned against assuming
that these chapters, which are approximately one sixth of the
volume, represent a complete analysis of the political system of
the International Typographical Union. There are many other
factors, not presented here, but dealt with in detail in the book,
that are important. This should, therefore, be read not as a total
interpretation of ITU politics, but rather as an example of
an effort to test empirically the implications of a macroscopic
sociological theory.—EDITOR.

negotiators in Paris in 1919 seemed to believe) that formal guarantees and written constitutions can insure democracy. The most carefully worded guarantees have been swept aside, and the most intelligent constitutions ignored, until now men seem liable to the opposite error of considering guarantees and constitutions worthless.

In few areas of political life is the discrepancy between the formal juridical guarantee of democratic procedure and the actual practice of oligarchic rule so marked as in private or voluntary organizations such as trade-unions, professional business associations, veterans' groups, and co-operatives. In fact, as many observers have noted, almost all such organizations are characterized internally by the rule of a one-party oligarchy. That is, one group, which controls the administration, usually retains power indefinitely, rarely faces organized opposition, and when faced with such opposition often resorts to undemocratic procedures to eliminate it. This is especially true of national organizations.

There is, however, one trade-union—the International Typographical Union (ITU), the organization of the men who set type in the print shops of North America—that does not fit this description. It is the only American trade-union in which organized parties regularly oppose each other for election to the chief union posts and in which a two-party system has been institutionalized. Since the beginning of this century the officers of the international union and of most of the larger locals have been chosen in biennial elections, in which two or more political parties have offered a complete slate of candidates for all offices. The two major parties of the union operate much as do the Democratic and Republican parties in American politics, though they have no connection with any group or party outside the union. The parties have been of roughly equal strength in the international since 1920, so that turnover in office occurs at least as frequently as in national politics. In the thirty-five years since 1920 five incumbent presidents of the international have been defeated for re-election. In the New York local of the union, the largest local of the ITU, containing 10 per cent of the membership, seven out of the last thirteen elections have resulted in defeat for the incumbent president. Probably nothing like this has happened in any other trade-union or in any other "private government" (as we may call voluntary organizations) anywhere in the world.

The Theory of Oligarchy

The pattern that characterizes almost all private organizations was generalized over forty years ago by the German sociologist, Robert Michels, when he laid down his famous "iron law of oligarchy" in the following terms: "It is organization which gives birth to the dominion of the elected over the electors, of the mandataries over the mandators, of the delegates over the delegators. Who says organization says oligarchy."[1]

The experience of most people as well as the studies of social scientists concerned with the problem of organization would tend to confirm Michels' general-

[1]Robert Michels, *Political Parties* (Glencoe, Ill.: Free Press, 1949). This book was first published in Germany in 1911.

173

ization. In the myriad nominally democratic voluntary organizations, men have learned that the clauses in the constitutions that set forth the machinery for translating membership interests and sentiments into organizational purpose and action usually bear little relation to the actual political processes that determine what their organizations do. At the head of most private organizations stands a small group of men most of whom have held high office in the organization's government for a long time, and whose tenure and control are rarely threatened by a serious organized internal opposition. In such organizations, regardless of whether the membership has a nominal right to control through regular elections or conventions, the real and almost invariably permanent power rests with the men who hold the highest positions. And this is as true for trade-unions as for other private organizations.

Occasionally the criticism of oligarchic control within the labor movement leads to successful attempts to democratize the constitutional structure of unions so as to reduce the power of the officials: the election of officers at conventions is replaced by a direct membership vote, referendums are required for constitutional changes, members are enabled to initiate referendums directly. But with very few significant exceptions all the efforts to reduce oligarchic control by formal mechanisms have failed. In those cases where an entrenched oligarchy was finally dislodged the new leaders soon reverted to the same tactics they had denounced in the old. Even anarchist political and labor groups, which one might expect on the basis of their ideology to be highly sensitive to the dangers of oligarchy, have found it impossible to maintain an active democracy. In pre-Franco Spain and in other countries where the anarchists had large organizations, a small semi-permanent group of leaders maintained itself in power and selected its own replacements. There is no more persuasive illustration of the unanticipated consequences of men's social actions than the recurrent transformations of nominally democratic private organizations into oligarchies more concerned with preserving and enhancing their own power and status than in satisfying the demands and interests of the members.[2]

What are the factors that account for the lack of democracy in labor unions? Why do opposition groups find it so difficult to survive? Michels and others who have dealt with the problem have summed it up in large generalizations: The nature of large-scale organizations is such as to give the incumbent officials overwhelming power as compared with that of the opposition; the situation of the leaders of most unions is such that they wish to stay in office and will adopt dictatorial tactics to do so; and the relation of the members

[2]It is, of course, true that the leaders' objectives of personal power and permanent tenure need not conflict with the needs of the members. Most voluntary organizations do in fact represent their members' interests in conflicts with other groups. But there may arise a situation in which the needs and goals of the leaders or simply their desire for peace and quiet in office lead them to oppose or not fight for membership objectives. In an organization in which the members cannot vote on alternative procedures or courses of action it is impossible to know whether a leadership decision is in fact something the members desire.

to their union results in a low level of participation by the members.[3]

The fact remains, however, that the democratic political system of the International Typographical Union does exist. Indeed, the party system of this union has lasted for half a century, and regular political conflict in North American printing unions can be dated back to 1815. Up to now almost all analysts of the political system of "private governments" have devoted their energies to documenting further examples of oligarchy. From the point of view of the further development of social research in the area of organizational structure, however, cases that operate in ways not anticipated by theory supply the most fruitful subjects for study. The analysis of such deviant cases—by refining the theoretical structure of empirical studies—can increase the predictive value of their findings. In other words deviant case analysis can and should play a *positive* role in empirical research, rather than being merely the "tidying up" process through which exceptions to the empirical rule are given some plausibility and thus disposed of.[4]

---

[3]These factors have been discussed in considerable detail in another publication by the senior author of this essay. See Lipset, "The Political Process in Trade Unions: A Theoretical Statement," Morroe Berger *et al.*, *Freedom and Control in Modern Society* (New York: Van Nostrand, 1954), pp. 82–124. Cf. also Philip Selznick, "An Approach to a Theory of Bureaucracy," *American Sociological Review*, 8:1 (February 1943), 47–54.

[4]Patricia Kendall and Katherine Wolf, "The Analysis of Deviant Cases," Paul F. Lazarsfeld and Frank Stanton, eds., *Communications Research, 1948–1949* (New York: Harper, 1949), p. 153.

In the course of our analysis of the ITU we have systematically looked for the various *oligarchic mechanisms*—elements and processes that Michels and others found operative in the organizations they studied. Many of these mechanisms—for example, the monopolies of communications channels, which the officials of most unions ordinarily possess—are not found in the ITU, or, if present, their effects are greatly mitigated by other elements in the system. A large part of our analysis is directed at specifying those elements in the structure of the ITU and in the printing industry that work against oligarchic mechanisms and at spelling out the processes by which they contribute to the maintenance of the union democracy. And as we look for those attributes and patterns in the ITU that work to nullify the oligarchic tendencies present in large organizations, we are implicitly or explicitly setting forth the conditions necessary for the maintenance of democratic politics within private organizations.

A Theory of Democracy

The problem of democratic or oligarchic political institutions may be approached from two vantage points. We may ask what are the conditions that are responsible for the development and institutionalization of oligarchy, or alternatively, we may ask under what conditions democracy arises and becomes institutionalized. Almost all the literature that deals with political institutions in private government deals with the determinants of oligarchy. We have found only one article that raises the question of under what conditions democracy, that is, the institutionalization of opposition, can exist in voluntary organizations.[5] There is of course a voluminous literature discussing democracy as a system of civil government, but we must ask ourselves whether a variable that seems related to the existence of democracy in a political state is relevant to the existence of democracy in organizations.

Aristotle, for example, suggested that democracy can exist only in a society that is predominantly middle-class. In essence he and later theorists argue that only in a wealthy society with a roughly equitable distribution of income could one get a situation in which the mass of the population would intelligently participate in politics and develop the self-restraint necessary to avoid succumbing to the appeals of irresponsible demagogues. A society divided between a large impoverished mass and a small, favored elite would result either in a dictatorship of the elite or a dictatorship of demagogues who would appeal to the masses against the elite. This proposition still appears to be valid. Political democracy has had a stable existence only in the wealthier countries, which have large middle classes and comparatively well-paid and well-educated working classes. Applying this proposition to trade-union government, we would expect to find democracy in organizations whose members have a relatively high income and more than average security, and in which the gap between the organizational elite and the membership is not great.

A second proposition that has been advanced about

[5] Selznick, "The Iron Law of Bureaucracy," *Modern Review*, January 1950, pp. 157–65.

democracy is that it works best in relatively small units, in which a large proportion of the citizenry can directly observe the operation of their governments:[6] for example, the small Greek city-states, the New England town meetings, and the Swiss cantons. While historical research has indicated that much of the popular mythology about the democratic character of these societies is untrue, it is probably true that the smaller a political unit, the greater the possibility of democratic control. Increased size necessarily involves the delegation of political power to professional rulers and the growth of bureaucratic institutions. The translation of this proposition to the level of private government is clear: The smaller the association or unit, the greater membership control. There can be little doubt that this is true in the trade-union movement.

Both of these approaches to democracy, that in terms of internal stratification and that in terms of size, are somewhat unsatisfactory, however, as solutions to the problem of democracy in complex societies or large private organizations. Clearly democratic political institutions do exist in large, complex, and bureaucratically run societies and in societies that have wide variations in the distribution of income, status, and power. There is a third proposition about the conditions that

[6] Thomas Jefferson advocated "general political organization on the basis of small units, small enough so that all members could have direct communication with one another and take care of all community affairs." Cited in John Dewey, *Freedom and Culture* (New York: Putnam, 1939), p. 159. Cf. also Gunnar Myrdal, *An American Dilemma* (New York: Harper, 1944), pp. 716–19; John Dewey, *The Public and Its Problems* (New York: Holt, 1927), chap. 5; "The Federalist, No. 10," *The Federalist* (New York: Modern Library, 1937).

favor democracy that seems to be of greater value for our understanding of democracy in large private organizations. We know it under two names, the theory of political pluralism, and the theory of the mass society. Writers in English-speaking countries, trying to explain why democracy exists in these countries, have developed the theory of political pluralism. European writers, trying to explain why democracy is so weak in Germany and other countries, have developed the theory of the mass society. Both theories say in essence the same thing. They argue that in a large complex society, if the body of the citizenry does not belong to politically relevant *groups,* if it is "atomized," the controllers of the central power apparatus will completely dominate the society. Translated to the realm of the internal politics of private organizations, this theory suggests that democracy is most likely to become institutionalized in organizations whose members form organized or structured subgroups that, while maintaining a basic loyalty to the larger organization, constitute relatively independent and autonomous centers of power within the organization. Or, to put it in another way, democracy is strengthened when members are not only related to the larger organization but are also affiliated with or loyal to subgroups within the organization.

The Occupational Community of the ITU

This approach to the problem of democracy has been so attractive to us because, as a matter of fact, the ITU, in addition to its striking two-party system and internal democracy, is also characterized by a vast network of voluntary organizations created by its members to satisfy their social and recreational needs.

In most large ITU locals, such as those in New York, Chicago, and San Francisco, there are printers' social clubs, lodges, sport clubs, veterans' groups, and many other groups. On the international level there are three sports organizations of printers, for baseball, golf, and bowling. These hold annual tournaments to which teams and men come from different parts of North America. So numerous have voluntary local printers' organizations been that it has been impossible to compile an exhaustive list of all the printers' organizations that have existed in the last half century in New York City alone. Many had short histories or disappeared without leaving any records. More than one hundred fifty different organizations have been located without exhausting the sources, and we are certain that this list could be more than doubled.

The formal functions of most of the groups are primarily social. Some, at different times, have maintained regular headquarters where men could gather to talk or play cards, chess, or checkers and get something to eat and drink. Some are primarily sports organizations, though they may run occasional social affairs. Still others, such as the typographical societies, link their social affairs to benevolent activities. Some have brought together printers who are members of the same ethnic or religious group, such as the Dublin Society or the Jewish Printers. Union Label Clubs have enabled printers living in the same neighborhoods to come together to further union objectives. Common past experiences have been the basis for war veterans' posts or groups of former employees of defunct newspapers. In this bewildering variety trade and skill distinctions are another basis for grouping. Fraternal orders, such as the Masons, have also been the basis for printers' organizations.

Often within a single large printing plant, such as the large metropolitan newspapers, smaller versions sprout up of the groups that exist for the occupation as a whole. Veterans' posts, lodges, and social and athletic clubs composed of workers in the same plant are common. Some of the smaller shops or shifts often set up extravocational social or recreational units.

Until fairly recently regular weekly and biweekly newspapers were published, devoted largely to reporting the activities of the union and the various subgroups. Like the clubs, these newspapers had no official relation to the union itself and were published by private individuals. The most recent of these in New York, the *Typographical Forum* (1932–43), reached a peak circulation of 3500, or more than one third of the working members of the union. It ceased publication during the war, when there was not enough free time available to put out such a newspaper.

Social clubs, organized leisure activities such as bowling leagues, and union newspapers are of course not unique to the printers, although we know of no other occupation that has as many and as diverse forms of organized extravocational activities as the ITU. What is significant about the printers' "occupational community," as we will call this structure of clubs and other voluntary organizations and activities, is that it developed without any formal connection with the union. The various benevolent organizations, newspapers, social clubs, athletic teams, and lodges have for the most part been organized by working printers in their spare time.

The formal community of printers' clubs is paralleled by an informal one. That is, large numbers of printers spend a considerable amount of their leisure time with other printers. In interviews many printers reported that their best friends are other printers, that they regularly visit the homes of other printers, that they often meet in bars, go fishing together, or see each other in various places before and after work.

Without data on other workers it is difficult to judge whether there are more of these informal social relations among printers than there are in other occupational groups, but we suspect that just as the network of formal social activities is more extensive among printers than among other occupational groups, so, too, is the network of informal social relations.[7]

A number of factors are related to the existence of an "occupational community" among printers. (1) The high status of printing among manual occupations has the consequence of reducing printers' desires to associate with other manual workers who are lower in status. At the same time, the fact that printers *are* manual

[7] In a study of the extent of marriage within occupational groups Donald Marvin found that printers had the second-highest coefficient of marriage within the occupation among a large variety of occupations in Philadelphia. That is, holding constant the proportion of women in the trade, printers were practically at the top in the scale of occupational intramarriage. Donald M. Marvin, "Occupational Propinquity as a Factor in Marriage Selection," *Publications of the American Statistical Association,* No. 122 (June 1918), pp. 131–50.

workers lowers their chances to associate with middle-class individuals. Consequently printers are "forced" on each other for leisure-time associations. (2) The fact that printers like their work increases their desire to associate with each other. (3) A large proportion of printers work nights and weekends. This reduces their opportunities to associate with neighbors and other non-printers who work a more "normal" schedule. Night work is normally less demanding than day work and produces an atmosphere of greater camaraderie than the normal routine of day employment. (4) Most printers on entering the trade must serve a number of years as "substitutes," irregularly employed workers. In order to get employment during this period printers must spend a great deal of their non-working time "downtown" near the print shops, and consequently associate with others in the same situation.[8] (5) There is more socializing among printers on the job than in many occupations. On the large newspapers in particular the need to put out different editions means that there are long periods between editions in which men either have no immediate work or can arrange their work so as to stop and talk for a while.

Both management and the union administration have only a limited control over the men in the shops or their elected leaders, the chapel chairmen. Management's power is limited by the power of the union, which is made explicit in rules barring non-members

[8] In the larger work from which this essay is drawn, these hypotheses have been tested with quantitative data drawn from the interviews with a sample of the members of the New York union.

of the union from the floor of the print shop during working hours. The union officialdom's control over the members or chapel chairmen is minimized by the existence of strongly held union norms, which inhibit efforts by union leaders to punish men for their opinions or to influence the election of chapel (shop) officers. Thus both on and off the job, in clubs, in the print shops, and in informal get-togethers printers are engaged in a variety of informal social relations with each other.

Is it possible that these two major differences between the ITU and other unions, that is, the incidence in the ITU of a democratic political system and of an extravocational social system, are related, that the intraorganizational social relations operate in some way—perhaps together with other factors—to sustain the political democracy of the ITU?

In general we find that those men who are active in the printers' occupational community, whether informally or formally, are also those who are involved and active in the union.[9] Thus, of those printers who had the least to do in their social life outside work with fellow-printers, only 7 per cent were active in some way in union politics; while of those who had

[9]The ITU, despite its active political life, is no exception to the general rule that men will not attend meetings that do not concern them or are unimportant. Attendance at regular New York membership meetings that have no major issues on the agenda runs from two to five hundred, or between 3 per cent and 6 per cent of the membership. However, important meetings will have an attendance of between two and three thousand members, about one third of the membership. Meetings of this size occur two or three times a year.

most to do socially with fellow printers, 55 per cent were active in union politics.

Though this indicates that the printers who are socially active with fellow-printers are also more likely to be politically involved, the question remains, just what is the relation between the social activities of the printers' community and the active political life of the union? Before presenting the data we will describe here in more detail the theoretical approach, which suggests just what this relation is.

The Mass Society

The current interest in the relation between voluntary organizations and politics is an outgrowth of the concern with totalitarianism,[10] but one of the earliest efforts to specify this relation was made over 120 years ago by Alexis de Tocqueville while attempting to solve a problem comparable to the one that we are dealing with in this study. Tocqueville wanted to find out why the United States alone among the countries of his day had a successful and stable democratic political order. He pointed to the fact that, as compared with Europeans of his time, "Americans . . . constantly form associations."[11] Tocqueville then goes on to raise the

[10]See Emil Lederer, *The State of the Masses* (New York: Norton, 1940); Hannah Arendt, *Origins of Totalitarianism* (New York: Harcourt Brace, 1950); Max Horkheimer, *Eclipse of Reason* (New York: Oxford University Press, 1947); Karl Mannheim, *Man and Society in an Age of Reconstruction* (New York: Harcourt Brace, 1940); Philip Selznick, *The Organizational Weapon* (New York: McGraw-Hill, 1952); José Ortega y Gasset, *The Revolt of the Masses* (New York: Norton, 1932).

[11]Alexis de Tocqueville, *Democracy in America* (New York: Knopf, 1945), pp. 376–86, for this and the quotations below.

question, just as we have, "Is the coincidence of a democratic political system with a highly developed organizational life the result of accident? Or is there in reality any necessary connection between the principle of association and that of equality?"

Tocqueville concludes that the coincidence of democracy and such organizational life is not accidental:

When the members of an aristocratic community adopt a new opinion, or conceive a new sentiment, they give it a station, as it were, beside themselves, upon the lofty platform where they stand; and opinions or sentiments so conspicuous to the eyes of the multitude are easily introduced into the minds or hearts of all around. In democratic countries the governing power alone is naturally in a condition to act in this matter; but it is easy to see that its action is always inadequate, and often dangerous. A government can no more be competent to keep alive and to renew the circulation of opinions and feelings than to manage all the speculation of productive industry. No sooner does a government attempt to go beyond its political sphere and to enter upon this new track, than it exercises, even unintentionally, an insupportable tyranny; for a government can only dictate strict rules, the opinions which it favors are rigidly enforced, and it is never easy to discriminate between its advice and its commands. Worse still will be the case if the government really believes itself interested in preventing all circulation of ideas. . . . Governments, therefore, should not be the only active powers; associations ought, in democratic nations, to stand in lieu of those powerful private individuals whom the equality of conditions swept away. . . .

Nothing, in my opinion, is more deserving of our attention than the intellectual and moral associations of America. The political and industrial associations of that country strike us forcibly; but the others elude our observations, or if we discover them, we understand them imperfectly, because we have hardly ever seen anything of the kind. It must, however, be acknowledged that they are as necessary to the American people as the former, and perhaps more so. In democratic countries the science of association is the mother of science; the progress of all the rest depends upon the progress it has made. Among the laws that rule human society there is one that seems to be more precise and clear than all others. If men are to remain civilized, or to become so, the art of associating together must grow and improve in the same ratio in which the equality of conditions is increased.

In the same chapter in which he discusses associations Tocqueville goes on to discuss a further condition of democratic politics in complex society, the need for a means not controlled by the state through which ideas and information may be presented to thousands of people at once. In democratic society he sees this need met by the existence of the newspapers.

The effect of a newspaper is not only to suggest the same purpose to a great number of persons, but also to furnish means for the execution in common of the designs which they may have singly conceived. The principal citizens who inhabit an aristocratic country discern each other from afar; and if they wish to unite their forces, they move toward each other drawing a multitude of men after them. It frequently happens on the contrary in democratic countries, that a great number of men who want to combine cannot accomplish it, because they cannot see, and know not where to find, one another. A newspaper then takes up the notion or the feeling that had occurred simultaneously, but singly, to each of them. All are then immediately guided toward the beacon; and these wandering minds, which had so long sought each other in darkness, at length meet and unite.

Large national associations, too, find "means . . . to converse every day without seeing each other, and to take steps in common without having met. Thus hardly any democratic association can do without newspapers." In fact, "a newspaper . . . always represents an association that is composed of its habitual readers."

Voluntary associations thus serve two needs of a democratic society. They are a source of new opinions independent of the state and a means of communicating these new suggestions to a large section of the citizenry. Two other important functions are the training of men in the skill of politics and the consequent increase in their actual participation in political organizations. Men who "never acquired the habit of forming associations" will not learn suddenly to do so because a crisis has occurred. "The greater is the multiplicity of small affairs, the more do men, even without knowing it, acquire facility in prosecuting great undertakings in common." Or, as Émile Durkheim put it:

A [democratic] nation can be maintained only if, between the states and the individual, there is intercalated a whole series of secondary groups near enough to individuals to attract them strongly in their sphere of action and drag them, in this way, into the general torrent of social life.[12]

[12]Émile Durkheim, *The Division of Labor* (Glencoe, Ill.: Free Press, 1947), p. 28.

A union can be considered, of course, one of those necessary secondary organizations within society, one of the mediating organizations between the individual and the state. But here we consider it as a social system in its own right, and ask whether *within* this social system we have a state of the masses or the kind of complex, articulated structure that, according to this theory, is necessary to support democracy. Most large unions and many other associations approximate the state of the masses in their lack of mediating organizations between the administration and the individual members. The average large trade-union contains only one formal organization, the union apparatus itself, and a mass of individual members. There are no autonomous suborganizations that can function as centers of opposition or as independent sources of organizational communication. It is perhaps paradoxical that the very organizations that allow workers to act collectively in their relations with employers are ordinarily so contructed that *within* them the members are usually unable to act collectively in dealing with their leaders. But it is obvious, too, that there is a limiting size below which organizations can act democratically without any groups mediating between the members and the associations. In our judgment, this limit is determined by the possibilities of communication. As long as an individual can reach every member of a group personally and the group is small enough for men to know and judge the work and policies of their leaders through firsthand observation, democracy can flourish. And, in fact, many small union locals are highly democratic. (Small unions also cannot usually

190

give their leaders much income or social status, so the leaders are less tempted to maintain power by restricting democracy.)

There is one further qualification to the description of trade-union members as a mass of isolated individuals. Actually there is one mediating group within large union locals, the shop organization. The extent to which this group can operate as a politically significant secondary group is limited, however, by the communications system. In most one-party unions the only means of communication between shops or with the union administration is through the bureaucracy of the organization itself. A shop group is also usually dependent on the officers of the union for support against the employer and thus ordinarily cannot constitute a basis for organized opposition. In the ITU, however, the shop organization and its officials have a great deal of autonomy vis-à-vis the local or international officers. This pattern is in part related to the fact that shop organization existed before the union was formed. Its perpetuation can be tied to the decentralization of the printing industry and, perhaps even more important, to the democratic system itself, for the shops are able to protect themselves from encroachments from the union officers by their power to defeat an administration in the next biennial election.

Up to now we have spoken of the functions of secondary organizations for a democratic society or private government. Superficially similar organizations exist in totalitarian societies, but their function is quite different. The totalitarian leader wants the citizens to attend meetings, read political literature, listen to broadcasts, and belong to and be active in age, occupational, sports, and various other groups, since by this means he can reach them with his point of view. Similarly, some trade-unions, especially those under Communist control, have made strenuous efforts to increase interest in the union by establishing various forms of union-controlled leisure-time organizations and making attendance at union meetings compulsory. It is fairly obvious that Communist labor leaders are not anxious to encourage and deepen internal democracy in their unions, but rather recognize that by multiplying the controlled activities of their members they are increasing their own chances to reach and indoctrinate the membership and so reducing the possibility that it will develop hostile attitudes and withhold support in a crisis situation. As a general hypothesis, one might suggest that the greater the changes in the structure of society that a governing group is attempting to introduce, or the greater the changes in the traditional functions of unions that a union leadership is attempting to effect, the more likely the leadership is to desire or even to require a high degree of participation in various groups by citizens or members. The radical changes that accompany social revolution, or on a smaller scale the transformation of a trade-union into a political weapon, put severe strains on group loyalties and create a potential for strong membership hostility toward the leadership. A high level of controlled and manipulated rank-and-file participation is perhaps the only way, given the leadership's purpose, of draining off or redirecting the discontent created by violent changes in traditional patterns and relations.

It should be noted, however, that many non-totalitarian movements and organizations also attempt to encompass the total life of their membership. Ever since the Catholic Church has been threatened, either by anti-clericalism and secularism in Catholic countries or by opposing religions in other countries, it has established networks of unions, lodges, social groups, youth groups, and other associations to prevent Catholics from being exposed to values and associations that may threaten their religious beliefs. Similarly, the Social Democratic parties of Europe, especially those of Germany and Austria, built the first total political environment, which in many ways resembled that of the Catholic Church. A number of political observers have suggested that the efforts of the Communists and Nazis to involve completely their members and supporters in activities bound to the party were modeled on the practices of the Catholics and Social Democrats. In this country a number of trade-unions led by present or former socialists have made similar although less successful efforts.

It is important, therefore, to differentiate between communities or associations that have consciously organized the daily lives of their members through a variety of groups that are linked to themselves and groups formed in relative independence of the central authority. Both situations will probably lead to a high level of participation in the affairs of the community or of organizations. The first situation, however, will be negatively related with political democracy, while the latter is one of the requirements for the institutionalization of democracy.

These facts suggest the following paradigm of the relation between extrapolitical association and the nature of government.

A. *Non-existence of secondary organizations* (that is, a mass society) *helps maintain*

    a conservative oligarchy, such as is found in South American dictatorships, in Europe before the nineteenth century, or in the average stable American trade-union

B. *Existence of secondary organizations*

    (1) *controlled* by their government helps maintain *revolutionary totalitarianism,* intent on making changes within the society which it governs, as in Nazi Germany or Soviet Russia

    (2) *independent* of the government helps in maintaining *democracy,* such as is found within the ITU or in the United States or most European democracies

To recapitulate: It is suggested that democratic politics necessarily rest on a multitude of independent organizations, the manifest functions of which need not be political. Such organizations serve in society as a whole or in unions (1) as arenas within which new ideas are generated; (2) as communications networks through which people may learn and form attitudes about politics; (3) as means of training potential opposition leaders in the skills of politics, and of thereby attaining the status necessary to become political leaders; (4) as one of the principal means of getting individuals to participate in the larger political arenas; and (5) as bases of opposition to the central authority.

The necessary characteristics of such independent organizations, according to this theory, are clear. They must be able to mediate between the individual and the state, or union, which means that: (1) They must have sources of power *independent* of the central body. Of course, this power can be of several kinds. The political power of the church, for example, resides in its popular support plus the existence of strong cultural sentiments protecting it from interference, while that of an organized gambling syndicate is completely different. (2) The power of these groups relative to the central body must be considerable. A nation or a union that is composed entirely of very small communities, isolated except for communication through government or central union channels, would be nearly as atomized as separate individuals as far as any possibility of democratic political opposition or collective action is concerned. Within the ITU itself, as distinct from its local affiliates, the large urban locals that have been able to maintain considerable autonomy serve as independent sources of power in international union politics, and generate both leaders and organizational facilities for an opposition party. This pattern, like the autonomy of the shop within the locals, is a consequence both of the printing industry's decentralization and of the democratic party system.

We must distinguish between two very different functions of secondary organization. On the one hand, they act as bases of countervailing power,[13] as interest groups restraining the absolute power of the central body. On the other hand, they serve to increase political participation. Now the exercise of power and the

[13]See John K. Galbraith, *American Capitalism: The Concept of Countervailing Power* (Boston: Houghton Mifflin, 1952).

encouragement of political participation are such different functions that rather different social organizations may perform them. It is possible for a society to have a wide variety of secondary associations, which play the important role of countering the power of the state, and not have an underlying structure of primary groups to provide the second function of increasing personal involvement. In some respects we may think of urban society in the United States as being a mass society in this sense. Social relations *within* the groups that exercise important pressure in politics are often attenuated. Groups such as veterans' associations, automobile clubs, consumers' co-operatives, medical plans, and the typical trade-unions all operate to maintain democracy in the larger society by acting as independent bases of power, while few of their members attend meetings or engage in informal social relations with other members.[14]

[14]Two students of voluntary organization have summed up the available evidence on participation in such groups as follows:

"In the 'service clubs,' for example, there is a very active nucleus and a large group who are 'just members': . . . The American Legion was founded in 1919 by a small group . . . and is run by a self-perpetuating oligarchy. . . . Goldhamer summarized the situation for fraternal organizations as follows: 'Though fraternal organizations are subject to democratic control, it appears that the actual formulation of policy . . . is largely the function of a few interested individuals with the great hulk of the membership acquiescing as long as these policies do not interfere with their private lives.' The Consumer Cooperative Movement, which stresses equal and active participation by all members more than most other associations do, is no exception to the active minority pattern. . . . Even in avowedly activist organizations, there is minimal participa-

In this respect the ITU is different; its suborganizations are often capable of performing both functions. Compared to most trade-unions and important political units, the ITU is quite small; the total membership in the United States and Canada is only about 100,000, of whom 10 per cent are in the New York local. Therefore, organizations within the unions are usually of a size that will permit them to carry out both the function of countervailing power and that of motivating members through primary group contact. A club or print shop can be small enough to maintain a high degree of contact among its members and at the same time be large enough relative to the administration to give prestige to opposition leaders recruited from it and to defend the rights of individual members. Of course, in relation to the international union a club or a single print shop is not likely to have such power. But on this level the union's political parties and the

tion. . . . In the most powerful and deeply rooted People's Organizations known in this country the degree of popular participation reached a point varying between five and seven per cent!" Bernard Barber, in Alvin Gouldner (ed.), *Studies in Leadership* (New York: Harper, 1950), pp. 484–85.

"In McKean's study of interest groups in New Jersey he repeatedly notes cases in which activity is confined to a few individuals in a group. In the National Association of Manufacturers, even among those belonging to the key policy-making bodies, participation varies widely. It is estimated that less than half the board members regularly attend meetings and that committee attendance is even lower. In the medical societies lack of participation has been a matter of some concern to the active elements from the very beginning. A similar situation has characterized labor unions, especially at the local level." David Truman, *The Governmental Process* (New York: Knopf, 1951), p. 154.

large locals appear to play the necessary role of counteracting central administrative power.

THE OCCUPATIONAL COMMUNITY AND THE POLITICAL SYSTEM

We will now approach empirically the question of this relation between the printers' social community and the ITU's political system by way of our data, which consist of interviews and questionnaires conducted with a random sample of members and leaders of the New York local of the ITU. Formally there is no relation between the organized printers' community and the political system. The printers' clubs are explicitly non-political and even anti-political; in some cases officials of such groups refused to discuss their own political beliefs on the grounds that union politics had nothing to do with the social organizations. Yet a connection exists, as the following pages will document.

Earlier data showed that those men who are most involved in formal or informal relationships with other printers are also more likely to be active and interested in union politics. At the same time participation in the leisure activities of the occupational community is in large part determined by factors that are independent of the political system. These facts suggest the following process: After men enter the trade, some are motivated or even pushed into taking part in the occupational community. A high degree of interaction with fellow unionists in turn serves to motivate them to greater interest and participation in union politics.

The occupational community is of course not the only means by which individuals are stimulated to participate in union politics.[15] Generalized political interest or awareness and the specific political ideologies of men (liberalism, conservatism) prompt some participation in union politics. Some men also enter union politics to satisfy personal ambitions. The occupational community should be seen then as only one of a number of routes leading to similar behavior. These several processes are of course interrelated and tend to reinforce one another.

The Short-Term Process

Given the comparatively short period in which we could secure data from members of the union, it was necessary to test a number of our hypotheses on the process of involvement by examining what happened to the political activity and interest of the printers during a six-month period. The members of our sample of printers, all from the New York local, were interviewed in December 1951 and January 1952. About six months later, at the end of May, the same men were sent a questionnaire in which they were asked a number of questions concerning their activity and interest in the international election of May. About 70 per cent of the members of the sample returned their

[15]For example, Kovner and Lahne point out that the "higher degree of participation among the members of the ITU as against that of the pressmen is not related to the fact that the former can talk while they work, whereas press work discourages conversation." Joseph Kovner and Herbert J. Lahne, "Shop Society and the Union," *Industrial and Labor Relations Review*, 7:1 (October 1953), pp. 3–14.

questionnaires. Several of the interview questions concerning involvement in and knowledge of union politics were repeated in the May questionnaire. By examining the changes in response during an election campaign we can study the effects of participation in the occupational community on behavior in union politics.[16]

The questions asked allow us to examine changes in the level of knowledge between January and May. One such question was on the positions of the two union parties on signing the non-Communist Taft-Hartley affidavits. The Progressives, in power, opposed signing the affidavits; the more conservative Independents favored it. The difference in party politics was a major issue of the 1950 and the 1952 international election campaigns. An examination of the extent to which printers were aware of the opposition of the two parties to this over the period of the campaign is consequently a good test of the *communications* function of the printers' social community. In January twenty-two of our respondents who were active club members and one hundred sixty-eight who were inactive in clubs,

[16]Unfortunately the variation in method by which the two sets of data were collected affected the change of response to the same question. In answering questionnaires at home, men were more likely to admit low levels of interest and activity in the union than in the face-to-face situation of the interview. Many respondents, for example, told interviewers that they were "very interested" in union politics, but then in the following May election campaign indicated a lower level of interest. It is extremely unlikely that these men lost interest as a result of the campaign. We are forced to conclude, therefore, that as a result of the interview situation men conformed to democratic or union norms. As might be expected, however, the replies to questions eliciting *knowledge* of specific union issues were less affected by the shift from interview to questionnaire.

or non-members, were wrong in their conception of the position held on the Taft-Hartley affidavits by one of the two major parties; by May, 45 per cent of the first group and only 23 per cent of the second had shifted to a correct perception of this party's position.

Similarly, in January twenty-six active club members and eighty inactive ones were right in their view of this party's position; in May only 8 per cent of the first group and as much as 28 per cent of the second had backslid and were wrong in their perception of this party's position.

It is clear that the clubs not only had an effect in increasing the knowledge of those who did not know the correct answer in January; the active club members who were right during the interview were less likely to slip into an incorrect position in May.

Another question asked at both times concerned knowledge of issues between the parties. In January the men were asked, "What do you think are the major campaign issues between the Progressives and Independents?" In the May questionnaire we asked, "What in your opinion was the single most important issue of the recent campaign for ITU office?" Some of the men mentioned specific issues or differences, while others simply cited the personality of the candidates or could not give any issues. In answering the questionnaire, although there was no probing by an interviewer, more men mentioned issues or differences and fewer mentioned personalitites or failed to cite an issue. We can relate the degree of involvement in the occupational community to the proportion of men who changed from mentioning no issue or personality in

January to a mention of a campaign issue in May. Thus, if we consider those who could not think of a single issue in January, we find that:

86% of the active club members in this group,
42% of the inactive club members,
43% of the non-members,

were able to come up with one in May.

Similarly, again taking those who could not think of a single issue in January, we find that:

78% of those rated "high" in informal social relations,
49% of those rated "medium," and
28% of those rated "low,"

did, by May, have an issue in mind.

These figures show the remarkable difference that high involvement in either the formal or informal occupational community makes in seeing the issues of the campaign. And while active club members and those high in involvement in informal social relations with other printers were more likely in January to perceive more issues than those less active, the involved group was also more likely to increase its knowledge. In January, 56 per cent of the active club members mentioned an issue, as compared with 46 per cent of the other members of the sample. By May, however, 81 per cent of the active club members could name an issue as compared with 49 per cent of those who were not active in clubs.

It is significant to note that the middle group in the scale of informal relations was educated to the point of being able to name an issue to a much greater extent than the low group, while the middle group in club membership, the inactive members, did not differ from the non-members. This is just what we could expect, since this middle group in informal social relations has some degree of activity, while the inactive club members, being members in name only, would be no more exposed to the issues than the non-members.

Club members showed not only an increase in *knowledge* in the campaign; relative to the non-members they also showed an increase in interest and involvement in union politics. We asked these men in the January interviews, "During union election campaigns, do you talk about union affairs with your printer friends much, little, or never?" Again in the May questionnaire the same question was asked, except that this time the question began, "During this past union election campaign . . ." At both times more of the active club members reported talking "much" than did the inactive members or the non-members. Further, the analysis shows clearly that during the campaign it was the active club members who were most likely to shift from inactivity to activity.

The time between January and May in 1952 was not only the period of the union campaign but also one of mounting interest in national politics. The Republican and Democratic presidential primaries were being held during this period, and the national conventions took place a few weeks after the questionnaires were distributed and returned. In both January and May we asked the men, "Do you get more worked up about something which happens in national politics and public affairs or about something which happens in union affairs?" Men could answer "National," "Union," or "Both equally." Overall, the members of the union were more concerned with national politics, and between January and May more men shifted from replying, "Union politics" to "National politics." But among the active club members there was a greater shift toward concern with union politics than toward national politics, while among all others the shift was greater toward national politics.

The foregoing analysis documents one basic point: that, regardless of the manifest purposes of those who take part in the formal or informal activities of the occupational community, these activities do play an important role in increasing the knowledge of, and involvement in, union politics of previously inactive or relatively uninterested printers. These data, however, cover only a six-month period, and it is obvious that the factors that are related to such knowledge and activity are operative over much longer periods. It is reasonable to project the implications of our analysis and suggest a long-term process. New members of the union would on the whole be relatively ignorant of union affairs and uninterested in politics. After some time in the union they would be divided into two groups, those who became involved in the occupational community and those who did not. The first group would be more likely to get involved in discussions about union matters, meet people active in union politics, and gradually develop more knowledge and interest concerning union politics. Those who remained outside of the occupational community would be subject to less stimulation, would take longer to learn about the union and its politics, and as a group would remain less knowledgeable and interested. With the passage of time a larger proportion of the former group would become active in union politics and thus help to continue the system.

The Role of Ideological Sensitivity

How are we to account for those who, while deeply involved socially with other printers, are not interested in union politics, or who, while active in union politics, have few other social relations with printers? Both these groups are atypical, yet important for understanding the whole system. These men, we suggest, are to be understood principally in terms of the two factors of generalized political awareness and specific ideology.

Printers, like other men, differ in their orientation to politics. They vary in their sensitivity to matters of policy or ideology when they vote or take part in politics. Some men think largely in terms of policy differences or ideological differences, while other men's orientations to politics are based more on personal or other matters.

In order to distinguish these kinds of men we used answers to questions in which the respondents told what they thought union politics was about and why they favored one party or candidate more than another. If the questions were answered in ideological terms, that is, in terms of issues, the men were characterized as "high" in "ideological sensitivity." If they were answered in terms of non-policy matters, such as past specific failures of a party or attributes of its leaders, or with a failure to see any real difference between the parties, the men were characterized as low in ideological sensitivity. The sample was then divided into three operationally defined classes—high, medium, and low in ideological sensitivity.

When we consider the effect of this ideological sensitivity on the pattern whereby social relations stimulate an interest in union politics, we find an interesting result:

TABLE 1. Proportion Active in Union Politics, by Relative Ideological Sensitivity and Index of Social Relations

Index of Social Relations	Ideological Sensitivity		
	High	*Medium*	*Low*
High	61% (61)	42% (123)	26% (50)
Low	48 (33)	22 (88)	23 (53)

Note: The figures in parentheses in this and subsequent tables indicate the number of individuals on the basis of which the percentages have been calculated.

We see that those men who come out high on the index of social relations (the first line of Table 1), are, regardless of the degree of their political sensitivity, more active in union politics than those who come out low (the second line of the table). However, much of the effect of social relations in producing political involvement is to be explained by a single group, the middle group in the scale of ideological sensitivity: the men who neither see union politics wholly from an ideological viewpoint nor are completely insensitive to ideology. If the reader will examine the table, he will see that among this group—shown in the second column of the table—those who rate high on the index of social relations show a much higher percentage of men active in union politics than those who rate low— 42 per cent to 22 per cent.

On the other hand, when we consider the effect, not of social relations, but of the formal organizations of the occupational community, the printers' clubs, we find quite different results:

TABLE 2. Proportion Active in Union Politics, by Relative Ideological Sensitivity and Club Membership

Ideological Sensitivity

	High	Medium	Low
Member of Club	63% (35)	41% (64)	41% (22)
Not Member of Club	52 (58)	29 (146)	19 (86)

Here we see it is the group that is *low* in ideological sensitivity—the last column in Table 2—that seems most greatly affected by club membership (41 per cent of the men low in ideological sensitivity who are club members are politically active, while only 19 per cent of the men who are low in ideological sensitivity and not club members are politically active). These differences among the three groups of printers enable us to specify in much greater detail the way in which the occupation's social community operates to stimulate political interest and involvement.

The group that is lowest in ideological sensitivity or political concern is especially interesting since, apparently, informal social relations have no influence on their involvement in politics (see Table 1 above) while club membership seems to have a great deal of influence.

We can understand the differential effect of informal

and formal social relations on the group of low ideological sensitivity in the following way: In the ITU we would posit the hypothesis that attitudes toward union politics are one of the decisive factors that influence choice of friends. The group high in ideological sensitivity will most probably have friends who are comparable to themselves in orientation and in political interest. Members of the low group, on the other hand, are likely to have friends who, like themselves, are repelled by or are uninterested in politics. So we should not expect the printer friendships of the ideologically insensitive to affect their political knowledge or interest.

Formal relations (membership in clubs), however, have a great effect in stimulating political interest. But how do the ostensibly non-political clubs operate to increase the political involvement of apolitical union members? Apparently in this way: The club members are not a representative sample of the union's membership. They are disproportionately composed of members who are active in union politics. About one in every five club members is also a member of a union political party, a proportion that drops to one in ten for the union as a whole. Of the club members 21 per cent are high in ideological sensitivity, as compared with 13 per cent of those not belonging to such groups. And in addition to the active leaders and other members of the union parties there are many fellow travelers and non-party independents who are often active in union election campaigns.

Now union politics can be effectively kept out of the *informal* relations of men who share a lack of interest or downright antipathy for union affairs, and whose friendship may be, in part, based on this feeling. But talk about union affairs and politics cannot be so easily excluded from the social relations that develop in and around printers' clubs. The clubs, the men who are active in them, and the talk and activities in which they engage are relatively independent of the sentiments or desires of any given member. So the man who joins a glee club or a bowling team or a local printers' social club, or any other printers' organization unrelated to union politics, will find that a large proportion of its members are involved in and talk about politics. Men who do not get to union meetings or read political circulars may thus be exposed to political talk before and after the club meeting, while riding home on the subway, or while waiting to bowl.

Some findings in communications research and political behavior are relevant here. *Experimental* studies of the influence of educational broadcasts indicate that audiences can be greatly influenced by such efforts. Yet studies of *actual* listening habits of radio audiences indicate little positive effect of such programs, for the simple reason that the listening audience the educational broadcasts are designed to reach simply does not tune in. Once it can be made a captive audience, whether in experiments or through sugaring the educational pill, these programs have an effect. Similarly, in the ITU men come to the clubs for social reasons but thereby also become a captive audience for the political activities.

In *The People's Choice*, Lazarsfeld, Berelson, and Gaudet report that voters are more likely to be affected

209

by interpersonal contact, especially by political "opinion leaders," than by formal propaganda.[17] They also indicate that middle-class persons who belong to ostensibly non-political organizations such as women's clubs are more likely to be politically active than those who do not belong to such groups. Among workers, however, only membership in trade-unions had the same effect. The analysis of the effect of printers' clubs suggest a possible explanation of these findings. Given the known fact that a larger proportion of middle-class persons than workers take an active interest in politics. one would expect middle-class clubs to contain more politically interested individuals than would most workers' social organizations. Consequently members of a middle-class group would more likely be politically stimulated than members of workers' clubs. If this is correct, then one should find in European countries, where the existence of a large labor political movement has stimulated the political interests of many workers, that workers would show the same tendency as middle-class individuals here.

In effect we are suggesting that increased contact among individuals who are politically active and those who are not increases the possibility that the latter will be politically stirred.

Thus far we have not discussed men who are *high* in ideological sensitivity. If we turn to these men, we find a puzzling phenomenon. Participation in printers' clubs makes for some difference in their political activity, but still less than among those who are low or in the middle on the scale of ideological sensitivity.

[17]See pp. 164–69, supra.—EDITOR.

Our initial efforts to explain this phenomenon rested on the assumption that if one is highly responsive to issues and ideas in politics, then the additional stimulation provided by social relations is not important. The printer with a strong ideological bent is motivated to participate in union politics. He had less need of the occupational community to inform him of issues and to awaken his political interests.

This interpretation, while plausible, still left unanswered questions. Given the assumption that these men are more likely to talk about politics than any other group in the sample, it was difficult to accept the finding that a high degree of involvement in the occupational community did not lead to greater involvement in politics.

When we pressed our analysis further, we did discover, for one group of men high in ideological sensitivity, that participation in the printers' social community had the expected effect. We had classified men as politically conservative or liberal on the basis of their answers to a given item scale of political attitudes on national issues, and, as we see in Table 3, among the group high in ideological sensitivity liberalism or conservatism *does* make a difference in participation in union politics.

TABLE 3. Proportion Active in Union Politics, by Relative Ideological Sensitivity and Political Bent

	Ideological Sensitivity	
	High	Medium or Low
Liberal	73% (41)	33% (113)
Conservative	31 (16)	29 (193)

The highly politicized conservative, who accepts many of the values of the middle-class or business community, is much less likely to be directly motivated to participate in union politics than the highly politicized liberal. Since their values are more nearly allied to those of the business community than those of militant unionism, these ideologically sensitive conservatives may even tend to dissociate themselves from union political activity.

Now it is among those conservatives who, while high in ideological sensitivity, are nevertheless active in union politics that we find the printers' social community playing a role. These men must be channeled toward political activity, and one way of doing this is through the occupational community. Although the small number of cases available for analysis precludes any definite statement, the data suggest that two distinct processes underlie participation in the occupational community and political activity for the ideologically sensitive man. Conservatives come to participate in union affairs through first participating in the nonpolitical occupational community, while liberals and radicals are motivated more directly by their values toward participation in union politics and are not dependent on social relations as an activating force.

It is now easy to understand the rather low participation in printers' clubs by the politically active ideological liberals. If men bring a strong concern with liberal or radical political issues with them to the union, they will early find an outlet for their interest in the activities of the union. For such men union politics is a highly satisfactory form of leisure-time activity.

The conservatives, on the other hand, are more likely to look first to the non-political social and athletic clubs for a social outlet if they seek their social satisfactions among printers.

It is thus not surprising that some of the ideological liberals were low in informal relations with other printers in spite of their being active in union politics. Some of them were active members of the American Labor, Liberal, or Socialist parties, or belonged to other general community groups that have political objectives. Their participation in union politics was only one aspect of a general concern with politics.

The political activation of the ideologically sensitive conservatives by the clubs indicates an important and previously unknown function of the occupational community. Since the leisure system recruits politically aware conservatives who might otherwise not be active in the union and its politics, it helps establish a balance between conservatives and liberals. It is significant, thus, that four of the conservative Independent Party leaders interviewed had served as presidents of printers' clubs before becoming active in politics. None of the more liberal Progressive Party leaders had come into union politics from this channel. They characteristically came up through the more directly political route of chapel chairman (shop steward) and party activity.

Conclusions

This essay dealt with the relation between participation in the occupational community and involvement in union political activity. The occupational community tends to make men more active politically than they would be in its absence. The clubs, especially, enable their members to learn the skills of politics by serving as officials and to build reputations throughout the union.

Though the clubs are non-political, the party leaders are aware of their political functions. One present party leader said that he first become involved in union politics while serving as president of an active printers' club with three hundred members. The president of the union appointed him a member of the union benefit board. Though this man was non-partisan at the time, he understood the reasons for his appointment, since "anyone who was a member of the benefit board was expected to help to get the president re-elected." A recent union president boasted to us of a political coup in getting the head of the printers' bowling league to serve as chairman of an important union committee. He pointed out that the man was well known throughout the union and in his capacity as head of the league was esteemed as a capable administrator.

Leadership in a printers' club is, however, only one of the means by which men become political leaders, and is much less important than direct political activity or involvement in shop political affairs. This is understandable, since outright partisans are rarely elected presidents of the non-political social clubs, and many men make careers out of club rather than union activity. The president of one of the printers' veterans posts was positively hostile toward discussing any questions about his union politics, since he felt that his role required him to be completely neutral. In fact, the clubs take particular care not to allow politics to be introduced in explicit terms. For the great majority of men the recreational and welfare activities that bring men together in the occupational community are sufficiently rewarding in themselves to make it important not to use the organizations openly for political purposes. The condition placed on political discussion seems to be that it must not threaten the manifest rewards of fellowship, recreation, welfare, and service.

The significance of the printers' clubs in helping to maintain the conditions supporting an institutionalized party system may be seen by comparing the situation in the ITU with other more typical, one-party unions. Occupationally limited social clubs are not unique to printers, though they seem more prevalent among them than among many other groups of workers. In fact, many unions spend a great deal of union money to create and maintain such groups. In a one-party union, however, there is clearly no need to keep them non-political, since there is no overt union politics; and these groups often become part of the communications system of the administration machine. Educational directors or other union officials attend club meetings and use the meetings as a means of reaching the membership with the administration viewpoint. In the ITU these clubs made it possible for an opposition to maintain itself, but this is true only because there are two legitimate parties and because the clubs have autonomous existence, and are not fostered by the union administration. Independent non-political clubs facilitate the existence of an opposition, and this existence of opposition in turn facilitates the political independence of the clubs.

It is possible to imagine that a two-party system and institutionalized democratic political procedures might exist in the ITU in the absence of these craft-linked independent organizations, or of even extensive informal social relations. The several functions that the occupational community fulfills for the political system are paralleled and duplicated by other institutions. The autonomous union-shop political structures might by themselves provide a sufficient base for an opposition political party. Or an opposition party with finances or motivation provided by outside groups and loyalties, such as the Association of Catholic Trade Unionists or various radical political parties, could by itself offer sufficient competition to the administration's control of the organs of information and opinion. Informal social relations on the job might, independently of leisure-time relations, provide contexts in which a proportion of the rank and file could be stimulated to active involvement in the union's affairs.

But what is a sufficient base for an opposition party in trade-unions? How much partisan activity would constitute "sufficient" competition in the market place of ideas? What is the degree of rank-and-file interest and involvement required to support democracy in a union? In short, what are the minimum functional requirements for internal union democracy? In this paper we have had the space to deal with only some of the factors that seem to be related to the perpetuation of a democratic opposition-party system. But even a complete specification of the structural factors that differentiate the ITU today from other unions would not answer the question of whether or not democracy is a necessary result of a particular cluster of such factors. To deal thoroughly with the problem of the unique character of the ITU'S political system a detailed historical analysis would be necessary. This analysis is presented in *Union Democracy*. There we attempt to show that the existence of democracy in the ITU today is in large part the result of converging events occurring over a number of decades, each of which contributed to the continuing stability of the system.

On the basis of the data presented here, however, we can say that the independent printers' organizations clearly work counter to the structural mechanisms that Michels considered to be inherent in large organizations. The secondary associations that Tocqueville saw as necessary for a democratic system exist in the ITU; and these groups support its party system—the ITU's most striking contribution to the trade-union movement.

Suggestions for Further Reading

ROBERT MICHELS. *Political Parties* (Glencoe: Free Press, 1949). The classic study of the internal structure of voluntary associations, dealing primarily with pre-World War I European socialist parties.

V. L. ALLEN. *Power in Trade Unions* (London: Longmans, Green, 1954). An effort to relate trade-union government in Britain to the larger problem of representation and democracy in society at large.

DAVID TRUMAN. *The Governmental Process* (New York:

Alfred A. Knopf, 1951). A large part of this book contains a systematic analysis of the factors affecting the political life of voluntary associations.

OLIVER GARCEAU. *The Political Life of the American Medical Association* (Cambridge: Harvard University Press, 1941). An excellent study of the power structure within the A.M.A.

S. M. LIPSET. "The Political Process in Trade Unions: A Theoretical Statement," Morroe Berger *et al.* (eds.), *Freedom and Control in Modern Society* (New York: Van Nostrand, 1954), pp. 82–124. An attempt to formulate propositions dealing with the political life of unions, and to suggest ways of testing them in research.

The Dynamics of Bureaucracy

PETER M. BLAU

A bureaucratic form of organization, according to Max Weber, is one that in the interest of optimum efficiency induces an impersonal and rational orientation toward all tasks.

The fully developed bureaucratic mechanism [he wrote] compares with other organizations exactly as does the machine with the non-mechanical modes of production. Precision, speed, unambiguity, knowledge of the files, continuity, discretion, unity, strict subordination, reduction of friction and of material and personal costs—these are raised to the optimum point in the strictly bureaucratic administration. . . .

Its specific nature . . . develops the more perfectly the more the bureaucracy is "dehumanized," the more completely it succeeds in eliminating from official business love, hatred, and all purely personal, irrational, and emotional elements which escape calculation.

Of course Weber did not mean to imply by this stress on official regulations that the behavior of an organization's members corresponds precisely to its blueprint. But since he was not concerned with this problem, he omitted from his analysis the way the actual operations of a bureaucratic structure are influenced by the unplanned elements that arise in it.

These emergent factors have been emphasized in most recent studies of organization. Chester I. Barnard, for instance, held that "personal contacts and interactions" always develop within what he termed "formal organizations," and that the resultant "informal organizations are necessary to the operation of formal organizations as a means of communication, of cohesion, and of protecting the integrity of the individual." Barnard's point was not merely that behavior and relations ordinarily fail to conform exactly with formal prescriptions—which would hardly be a novel discovery—but that the consistent pattern of this failure shapes the organization, which is thus not a static representation of its original conception but an ever-changing structure. In line with this theory this study presents an intensive analysis of one department of a state employment agency.[1] All consistent patterns of behavior and social interaction, whether based on the agency's official rules or their regular violation, were taken to be part of the bureaucratic organization and a reflection of its dynamic character.

Data do not speak for themselves, but only answer to the questions the investigator puts to them. Functional analysis, particularly the variant developed by Robert K. Merton, has been used to organize the data of this study. According to the basic tenet of this theoretical orientation, sociological inquiry is concerned, not only

[1]The larger work of which this is an abridgment includes also a comparative analysis of a federal law-enforcement agency.

with the purposes of social phenomena, but also with their consequences, and specifically with their contribution to the continued functioning of the social structure under observation. Thus, for example, the statistical records that provide administrators with accurate information about the operations of their subordinates are intended to improve the efficiency of operations. A functional framework directs attention to the actual consequences of such a supervisory system. These are likely to be of two types—not only the intended consequences, or what Merton has termed *manifest functions,* but also *latent functions,* or those unanticipated consequences of social behavior that contribute to structural adjustment. The existence of an exact record of their performance encouraged employees' attempts to improve their work on their own initiative, and therefore reduced the amount of criticism their superior had to offer; thus, as a latent function of these performance records, more cordial relations developed between the supervisor and her subordinates.

Merton's theoretical framework includes also the concept of dysfunctions, or observed consequences that lessen the system's adjustment to internal or external strains. The introduction of statistical records in the agency, to continue the same example, generated a competitive spirit among the employees that made it more difficult for some of them to complete their tasks. Dysfunctions are particularly significant in that they frequently indicate potential modifications of the structure. The statistical records, an innovation introduced to cope with one recognized defect in the organization, evoked new practices and interpersonal relations that themselves modified the departmental structure.

The central thesis of this study is that bureaucratic structures continually create conditions that modify these structures. In the study of larger social systems it is now generally recognized that developmental processes must be taken into account; but bureaucracies are still often regarded as rigid and static. Like all social structures, however, bureaucracies develop the seeds, not necessarily of their own destruction, but of their continuous transformation.

The Rules and Their Interpretation

This study was made in 1949 in the division of a state employment agency serving the clothing industry of a large Eastern city. The major responsibility of this agency, according to its training manual, was "to serve workers seeking employment and employers seeking workers." Employers telephoned in requests for workers; job applicants were interviewed to determine their qualifications and were referred to suitable openings.

Department X, the one under intensive investigation, was one of four in this division; it had twenty-four members—a department head, three section supervisors, fifteen interviewers, and five clerks. Two of its four sections were responsible for unskilled occupations in the clothing industry, one for handicapped clients, and one for maintaining the files and other clerical tasks.[2]

[2] In this abridgment the discussion of Section C, which handled applications of handicapped clients, has been omitted.

Nine of the twenty-four employees were men, the others—including the department head and two of the three supervisors—were women. Most of the interviewers and two of the clerks had college degrees. Interviewers received an average salary of only $3000, clerks about $2300; most of them had been in the agency for more than five years.

After an initial period of general orientation the activities of the department were observed daily for over three months, and each member of the department was also interviewed at home. Of course it is not possible through a case study with such a small sample to determine systematically what the general significance of the observed practices may be, particularly for larger organizations. By such an intensive analysis, on the other hand, direct observation, the study of documents, and interviews can be co-ordinated to obtain a variety of systematic empirical data on any particular point, so that hypotheses that evolve from the empirical work can often be tested immediately.

The training of the agency's interviewers began with a general orientation, including lectures on the history of the agency, its service philosophy and policy of non-discrimination, personnel and promotion policies. Most of the training, however, concentrated on the duties of the interviewer. The trainee learned that requests for workers, upon being received from employers over the telephone, must be recorded on a form, the job order. The procedure for obtaining all the information needed to fill out the twenty-five categories on this form was fully explained and exemplified. The interviewer was taught a formula, "What? How? Why? What is involved?" as a device for remembering to include all relevant information in this description of the job. Two days of training were devoted to the use of the four-volume code book, which contained numerical codes for 29,000 occupations. A series of demonstrations showed how to match the information on the job order with that on the application form in order to select the client best suited for a given vacancy. The importance of occupational adjustment and training to those who need it was strongly emphasized by the training staff; interviewers were taught how to recognize a client's need for counseling, and were told about the two types of counseling the agency offered.

All recipients of unemployment insurance benefits were required to report periodically to the employment agency, and the interviewers were responsible for notifying the unemployment insurance agency whenever a benefit client refused a suitable job "without good cause." Such refusals, whether in the form of rejecting the interviewer's offer or of failing to report to the employer after accepting it, disqualified a client from receiving these benefits for some time. The exact meanings of legal terms such as "suitable job" or "good cause for refusal" were explained to trainees, and they learned when to send a notification to the unemployment insurance agency and how to process this form.

The procedures used in Department X, however, were quite different from those taught in the training course. Occupational codes were not used. The "job formula," a phrase often heard in the training period, was never mentioned. Application forms were rarely made out. Candidates for jobs were selected not from application files but from applicants in the office. Counseling was virtually prohibited.

That is, basic changes in the operating rules had occurred as they were transmitted from the agency headquarters down to department and section. Agency-wide rules had to be abstract in order to guide the different courses of action necessary to accomplish the agency's objective in diverse situations. Progressive specifications of procedure could be noted as one moved down the organizational hierarchy to the point of actual contact with clients.

The clothing industry in this city was characterized by alternative seasons of feverish activity and widespread layoffs, erratic variations in demand owing to changes in fashion, and standardization of occupational tasks. Employers wanted workers immediately or not at all, and thus they not only called the employment agency but also advertised the openings with street signs in front of their shops. Department X could serve its applicants only if it referred a qualified worker before a passer-by had been hired. There was no time to call in clients selected from the office file of applicants and, moreover, little need of a careful choice at the low level of skill. Thus workers were selected for referrals directly from the flow of incoming applicants, and the rules governing interviewing were modified in the interest of speed. In most cases a sentence or two describing the applicant's last job and the amount of his experience were sufficient, and the suitable job openings in the file could be explained to him in a few words. The average interview took only ten minutes.

These *adjustments* of the selection procedure, designed to achieve the objectives of the agency under the special conditions in Department X, had unanticipated consequences. The original procedure was intended not only to find suitable jobs for clients but also to select the best-qualified applicant among all those available for a job, while under the system as it developed the first client meeting minimum qualifications was usually selected. Sheer chance—the coincidence of the employer's request and the applicant's appointment with the interviewer—largely determined the client's likelihood of being placed, and his skill beyond the minimum qualifications did not appreciably improve his chances.

The agency administration judged the department's operations largely on the basis of the number of placements it made, because this was the primary criterion of the state legislature in setting its appropriations for the agency. Thus finding jobs for applicants and workers for employers was considered to be the only "real" responsibility of the department. Counseling was virtually abandoned: the supervisor's permission for counseling a client was required, and it was rarely granted.

Modifications of this type were instituted also by the office staff. Each interviewer sought to maximize his placements, since this factor counted heavily in the evaluation of his performance. Thus, if a client receiving unemployment benefits sought to refuse a particular job to which he could be sent, he was reminded that this might disqualify him for benefit payments. Once interviewers thought of this device to exert pressure on benefit clients, they were reluctant to write notifications in terms of the original purpose of this procedure—to supply information to the unemployment insurance office. This modification interfered with the stated goal of Department X, which was to help clients find jobs they wanted, not to conscript them. In the interest of this goal superordinate officials *amplified* the procedure. They emphasized that notifications should not be used to intimidate clients: the interviewer had to tell his clients that he could not disqualify them but only send notice of refusals to the insurance agency, which determined whether disqualification was warranted. That is, when the interviewers' concern with maximizing placements induced them to redefine the situation and modify their procedures, the resulting practices interfered with operations, and the superiors had to adjust the rules to these internal changes in what might be termed a countermodification.

Intermediate officials in the hierarchy did not always react to their subordinates' deviations by amplifying procedures to counteract them. Sometimes they made allowances for such practices or even justified them, thereby reinforcing them. Some of the factors that led to these alternative responses are indicated by the following example.

The clerk-receptionists were responsible for screening clients according to the occupations for which job openings were currently available. This was not a pleasant task. They had to tell many clients, some of whom needed jobs desperately, to leave and return at a future date. On the highest administrative level this reappointment procedure was defined only in general terms: "The renewal practice . . . is designed to bring workers into the office when needed. . . . Because of the highly seasonal nature of the [clothing] industry . . . dates assigned may vary from one week to four months." On the department level more specific rules had been established: Most occupations served by Department X were divided into two classes; applicants in one were told to return after thirty days, and those in the other after sixty days. On the third level the supervisor implicitly recognized the need for exercising discretion when setting reappointments and thus permitted earlier "due dates" than the one or two months set by the department rule.

All five of the receptionists, finally, interpreted this procedure liberally. They exercised discretion, frequently making appointments earlier than specified; and they occasionally passed for an immediate interview a client who, according to the rules, should have been sent home. A receptionist who refused badly needed help acted counter to the service philosophy of the agency and was likely to experience the aggression of some of the clients. By giving earlier reappointments than were required receptionists mitigated the pressure on them and improved their relations with applicants—that is, the public relations of the agency. The average contact at the reception desk of the one clerk who did not enjoy this duty lasted 0.6 minutes, that of the others varied between 1.2 and 1.5 minutes. This extra time constituted the cost of improving the public relations of the agency and the work satisfaction of the receptionist. For by exercising some discretion when setting these dates the receptionists could transform a routine, mechanical duty into an interesting social experience.

The receptionists' liberal interpretation of reappointment procedure did not interfere with operations directly, for it was operationally immaterial whether one or another of the clients who met the qualifications received any particular job. However, the discretionary power of the receptionist had two dysfunctional consequences: more clients than could be handled came to the office, and applicants did not receive equitable treatment. Two different superiors responded to these modifications in opposite ways. The supervisor made allowance for them, acknowledging that so many factors had to be taken into account when setting the dates for reappointments that no simple rule could be followed. The department head, on the other hand, established a clear-cut procedure and explained in her directive that the scarcity of job openings made it useless to interview clients more frequently and that the scarcity of personnel made it impossible. The supervisor was concerned with immediate operations, while the department head was responsible for attaining long-range objectives.

Statistical Records of Performance

Social scientists know that the process of collecting information on people's activities influences these activities. The presence of an observer in a work group affects the behavior they want to study, and the repeated interviews in a panel study of political attitudes increases the respondents' interest in politics.

Similarly, the agency's collection of data on the operations of its employees influenced their conduct, for the knowledge that their superior would learn how many clients they had interviewed and would evaluate them accordingly induced interviewers to work faster. This direct effect constituted the major purpose of such performance records: the supervisors wanted to know the number of interviews completed by each subordinate in order to take corrective action in case any of them worked too slowly. The fact that the very counting of interviews had induced them to work faster facilitated operations by making such corrective steps superfluous.

Until the beginning of 1948, or while jobs were relatively plentiful, the only operation recorded for each interviewer was the number of interviews per month. However, when the labor market became tighter, this single criterion had a detrimental effect on operations. In the interest of a good rating the interviewer tried to maximize the number of interviews and therefore spent less time than was needed during a period of job scarcity on locating openings for clients. This rudimentary statistical record interfered with the agency's objective of finding jobs for clients.

In March 1948, two months after a new department head was put in charge, she instituted new performance records with the following eight indexes for each interviewer:

(1) Interviews: The number of interviews held with job applicants

(2) Referrals: The number of clients sent out to apply for a job

(3) Placements: The number of such referred clients actually hired

(4) (2)/(1): The proportion of interviews that resulted in referrals

(5) (3)/(2): The proportion of referrals that resulted in placements

(6) (3)/(1): The proportion of interviews that resulted in placements

(7) Notifications: The number of reports to the unemployment insurance office of clients' alleged misbehavior

(8) Application forms: The number of forms filled in for job applicants.

While the number of job openings available was beyond the department's control, the proportion of these openings it filled provided an index of the effectiveness of its operations. Immediately after the introduction of these records the proportion of job openings filled through the agency increased from 55 to 67 per cent.

Statistical reports influenced operations by inducing interviewers to concentrate their efforts upon the factors that were measured and thus would affect their rating. Because of the percentage figures included in his record an interviewer had not only to place many clients but also to exercise care in selecting a qualified client for each job, for otherwise the proportion of his referrals that resulted in placements would have been low. This curbed the tendency to send out clients quickly and indiscriminately in the hope that a large number, though a small proportion, would be hired— which would have constituted inefficient service to both workers and employers. On the other hand, an interviewer's rating would not be improved by being overmeticulous and referring only perfectly qualified clients, for then the proportion of his interviews that resulted in referrals would have been low.

The interviewers reacted to the introduction of performance records with as vehement hostility as manual workers do to production quotas. For these white-collar workers this attitude was intensified by the fact that "working on production like in a factory" had negative status implications. Interviewers often protested that the "statistics" measured "quantity" but not "quality," but this complaint was not justified. The performance records measured not only the amount of work done (the number of interviews) but also whether certain objectives were accomplished (the number of placements) and whether this was done by prescribed methods (the proportional indexes). The records tended to include all the elements that superiors considered important, and their omission of a factor also influenced operating practices. Thus, since counseling interviews were not included in the departmental report, interviewers rarely asked permission to give one, for these time-consuming interviews would only have interfered with making a good showing on the record.

Performance records served several operational functions in addition to the major one of increasing efficiency:

1. They facilitated hierarchical control over the staff. For example, the use of the proportion of referred clients who were hired as one element in the evaluation of subordinates enforced careful selection more effectively than any rule could have, because it

was then in the interviewer's interest to exercise care in sending out clients to apply for jobs.

2. These records enabled superiors to institute changes in operations quickly and effectively. While new procedures are not always opposed, usually a period of adaptation is required before they become fully effective. By altering the performance record or the relative emphasis on various factors administrators could induce lower echelons to change their practices immediately.

3. The use of performance records improved the relations between supervisors and interviewers. It was the supervisor's responsibility to criticize subordinates whose work was inadequate, and such criticism was often resented. Even when performance records did not relieve the supervisor of this duty, as they sometimes did, they usually reduced the resentment it created. Instead of having to tell an interviewer that *he* considered his performance unsatisfactory the supervisor could place the onus on his record, which he could try to help him to improve.

In spite of these advantages supervisors on all levels held it impossible to judge all aspects of performance on the basis of these indexes alone: "You can't reduce a man to a statistic." For if evaluation were to be based entirely on statistical indexes, a supervisor's responsibility would have been reduced to the clerical task of applying a mathematical formula to a set of data. Not only would this have made his job less interesting, but it would also have undermined his authority over subordinates. The fact that three of the five elements in the civil-service rating were *not* based on statistical records preserved the authority of supervisors and thus their ability to discharge their duty of directing the work of interviewers. On the other hand, once the records were set up they could not be ignored without dysfunctional consequences. The preparation of performance records set up expectations; and if the supervisor disregarded them, he not only alienated the interviewer but also destroyed the effectiveness of the records as an incentive.

Indexes are never perfectly related to the phenomena they are designed to measure. Interviewers tended to think of maximizing their ratings as their major goal, sometimes at the expense of the objectives these idexes measured—a form of what Merton has termed "*displacement of goals* whereby an instrumental value becomes a terminal value." The interviewers avoided operations that would take up time without helping them to improve their record, such as interviewing clients for whom application forms had to be made out. The supplementary index introduced in order to curb such a tendency was not wholly effective; for if there are too many criteria, most will be disregarded and only a few considered as important. The interviewers wasted time—their own and the public's—on activities intended only to raise the figures on their record. For example, when a client was laid off for a few days, interviewers made out a job order and referred the client back to this same job. In this way they improved their number of referrals and of placements (and the corresponding proportional indexes) without having found a job for a client. If a client said he expected to return to his former job in a few weeks, sometimes an interviewer asked him to return to the office then and "referred" him to his own job.

Competition and Productivity

Department X inculcated competition. As one interviewer put it, "The statistics showing how many interviews and placements each person made are passed around to all interviewers. Of course, you look at them and see how you compare with others. This creates a competitive spirit." Though superiors emphasized that these statistical records were used not to "compare interviewers with each other, but only with standards," fluctuations in the labor market made it impossible to establish abstract norms of performance. Thus, as one explained, "Each month we look at the production, and the average becomes the standard." Consequently interviewers were indirectly compared and, in fact, direct comparisons were also made. The competition in the department was as sharp as that of salesmen pushing the same product in one territory, each trying to reach each potential customer before anyone else could. In other departments, which did not have common pools of job orders, each interviewer handled a different occupational category. The strain in interpersonal relations observable in Department X did not develop there, for interviewers competed to make the best record, but not for job openings.

Employers' requests for workers were received over the telephone throughout the day, and the telephone operators distributed them among all interviewers in the appropriate section. In Section A the order forms describing the job openings were kept in five boxes, located on the desks of five interviewers, and in Section B in two boxes, which were moved from desk to desk as needed. All of the interviewers in either section were entitled to place clients in all of the jobs available and tried to fill openings before anyone else could.

One interviewer gave the following account of the illegitimate competitive practices that had developed:

When you take an order, instead of putting it in the box, you leave it on your desk. There was so much hiding of orders under the blotter that we used to ask, "Do you have anything under your rug?" when we looked for an order.

You might leave an order you took on the desk, or you might leave one you pulled from a box on your desk, even though you made no referral. . . .

Or you might take an order only partially. You write the firm's name, and a few things; the others you remember. And you leave it on the pad of order blanks. You keep on doing this, and all these orders are not in the box.

You can do some wrong filling out. For instance, for a rather low-salary job, you fill out "experience required." Nobody is likely to make a placement on that except you, because you know that experience isn't required.

Or, if there are several openings on one order, you put the order into "referrals" [file category for *filled* job openings] after you made one placement. So you have a better chance of making the next placement than somebody else. Time and again, you see four, five openings on one order filled by the same person.

Indeed, in one case eight out of nine openings on one order had been filled by the same interviewer. This tendency to monopolize job openings forced interview-

TABLE 1. Competitiveness and Productivity in Sections A and B

Interviewers	Job Orders Received (1)	Referrals Made by Recipient (2)	Referrals over Job Orders (3)	Index of Competitiveness (4)	Number of Placements (5)	Productivity Index (6)
Section A:						
A-1	34	19	.56	3.9	100	.70
A-2	62	27	.44	3.1	70	.49
A-3	40	28	.70	4.9	139	.97
A-4	71	32	.45	3.2	101	.71
A-5	69	18	.26	1.8	65	.45
A-6	106	43	.41	2.9	87	.61
A-7	10	3	.30	2.1	56[a]	.39
Section B:						
B-1	16	7	.44	2.2	46	.53
B-2	58	19	.33	1.6	62	.71
B-3	51	15	.29	1.5	65	.75
B-4	17	7	.41	2.1	48[a]	.55
B-5	43	19	.42	2.1	84	.97
Section A.	392	170	.43	3.0	590	.59
Section B.	185	67	.36	1.8	289	.67

[a] Adjusted for absence from the office of more than five days. Because of these adjustments the figures in this column add up to larger sums than the two totals given for the sections.

ers to watch one another's movements, if not to hide orders, then to prevent others from doing so.

Not all interviewers were equally competitive, and in order to show the differences among them the author constructed an index—the extent in excess of chance expectations to which each interviewer used for his own clients the orders he had himself received from employers. While this index did not reflect all forms of competition, it did measure the most prevalent forms, and, since it was based on the records of official transactions, it was not affected by the concealment of illicit practices. If no tendency to usurp orders had existed, one seventh of the job openings in Section A (with seven members) and one fifth of those in Section B (with five members) would have been filled by the interviewer who received the order. The incidence of the much larger proportions shown in Table 1 reveals monopolistic practices.

Column (1): The base period was the first half of April 1949. The large differences among interviewers in the number of orders received were not accidental. The two members of the department friendly with the telephone operators received many calls, and others may have been more successful than their competitors in inducing employers to channel requests for workers to them personally.

Column (2): This is *not* the total number of referrals made by each interviewer, but only the referrals during the base period to those job openings he himself had received.

Column (3): For each interviewer the dividing of the figure in Column (2) by that in Column (1) gives the proportion of the job openings he received that he referred his clients to.

Column (4): Index of Competitiveness. In order to standardize the index the proportions in Column (3) were multiplied by the number of persons in the section—that is, by 7 and 5, respectively. The degree of competitiveness is indicated by the amount by which this index exceeds 1.0.

Column (5): For each interviewer this is the number of placements made during April 1949.

Column (6): Productivity Index. In order to make the two sections of the department comparable the number of placements listed in Column (5) was divided by the average number of openings available to each interviewer in each of the two sections.

The interviewers in Section A were more competitive than those in Section B (3.0 as against 1.8). Most of the interviewers attributed this difference to the personality of some of the members of Section A—their ambition, eagerness to please superiors, or competitive spirit. "There is usually one individual who starts it, who becomes a pace setter. Once it has started, it is too late. The others have to follow suit." That this explanation is inadequate, however, is indicated by the behavior of the most competitive interviewer. When statistical records made her superior performance public knowledge, she decided to work less, quite possibly in response to pressures the others had brought to bear upon her. At the same time the other members of Section A, while complaining about the unfair production standards she set, improved their own performance and stimulated her to work fast again and compete for an outstanding performance record. On the other hand, one or two individuals in Section B were also accused of having competitive tendencies, but their colleagues successfuly discouraged monopolistic practices. That is, the competition of one group and the co-operation of the other were social factors, calling for explanation in sociological rather than psychological terms.

Structural Differences between Sections

Interviewers competed in order to maximize their placements. How well did competitive tactics accomplish this purpose? As can be seen by comparing columns (4) and (6) of Table 1, competitiveness was related to productivity in Section A, but not in Section B. The more competitive interviewer in Section A made more placements; the more competitive interviewer in Section B did not. Since monopolizing jobs was an effective way of improving one's placement record only in one group, its members had a good deal more incentive to engage in such competitive practices.

The co-operative norms that had developed in Section B discouraged competitive practices by making them ineffective. Many comments by interviewers illustrate this point:

The advantage [of Section B over Section A] is that we never cover up orders. We always work together. Statistics tend to make people egocentric, making everyone work for himself. Through co-operation we try to equalize the placements various interviewers make and counteract the statistics.

We did many things. We co-operated noting which applicants were deadheads, who would not take jobs when sent out. We checked each other's placements, so that statsitics were nearly evenly divided. If I saw an applicant at another desk, and had an order for which he might qualify, I would take the order over there. Every applicant became your applicant.

Although these co-operative practices did not equalize productivity, they did make competitive monopolization of jobs ineffective as an instrument for improving it. When a new interviewer manifested competitive tendencies, he was penalized by being excluded from this network of reciprocal information, so that any advantage from hoarding jobs was neutralized by the lack of co-operation it provoked.

There were three conditions in the past of the two sections that might account for the emergence of co-operative norms in one group but not in the other. First, the rating practices of the two supervisors had differed. Second, only one of the groups had had an opportunity to develop a professional code of employment interviewing. Third, the degree of job security had differed at the time statistical records were introduced.

1. The supervisor of Section A relied heavily on performance records in evaluating the interviewers: "And here, in the production figures, is the answer to the question: How good are you? Here you see exactly how good the work you did was." Interviewers often mentioned the pressure this created "especially around rating time." The supervisor of Section B, on the other hand, surprised his subordinates when he rated them for the first time: he tried to judge the entire person and he gave good ratings. The difference in approach

found expression in their interaction patterns with sub-ordinates. In Section B the supervisor had many more contacts with the interviewers under him than did the head of Section A (sixteen, as compared with six, per interviewer per day); and he initiated a larger pro-portion of these contacts (62 per cent as compared with 48 per cent). For the more that statistical rec-ords are used for hierarchical control, the less must the supervisor take the initiative in his interaction with subordinates. Since their ratings were not primarily based on performance records, the members of Section B were less anxious about productivity, and this en-couraged the development of co-operative norms.

2. The least competitive interviewers in Depart-ment X were persons identified with professions that set standards of correct interviewing—for example, a former social worker and a prospective clinical psy-chologist. Their orientation induced these interviewers to strive for other goals than maximum productivity, goals that competitive practices did not help achieve. A similar orientation developed in Section B after the war, when large numbers of returning veterans needed occupational advice. Counseling and intensive inter-viewing had therefore been stressed at that time, and three of the section's current members had been trained then by a supervisor especially interested in these phases of operations. As one of them described this period:

When I first came here, in May 1946, it was like an all-day consultation; we discussed placements with each other all day long. Nobody asked you how many place-ments you made, then. The emphasis was on quality.

In contrast, the members of Section A had not received their induction training together, nor had they been trained at the time when intensive interviewing of returning veterans had been emphasized.

In this situation Section B developed a professional code of its own. It was considered most important to help each client find a job that interested him and to give him all the occupational advice he needed; and quick interviews were unacceptable, since they could not meet these objectives. Competitive practices were not illegitimate means toward desirable ends, but illegitimate means toward worthless ends. Co-operation was still contingent on the absence of acute anxiety over ratings and thus on the supervisor's evaluation system, but this group code would have made it difficult for any supervisor to judge performance mainly on the basis of production figures.

3. Finally, most members of Section A were on probation pending permanent civil-service appointments when the performance records were introduced. Their insecurity led them to strive to impress superiors with their outstanding performance. In contrast, all but one of the members of Section B were veterans, whose employment could not be terminated except for cause.

Differences in these three conditions—the evaluation practice of the supervisor, development of a common professional orientation, and employment security—gave rise to two dissimilar social structures. While productivity was negatively valued in one section, it became a central value in the other: outstanding productivity resulted in high status in Section A, but in low status in Section B. When one member of Section

B explained why she considered a certain colleague to be the best interviewer in her section, she inverted official performance standards: "He has more patience; also, he made fewer placements, which I thought was to his credit. The person who does the better job very often has fewer placements." The most productive interviewer in this section was least respected and least popular. On the contrary, the most competitive and most productive member of Section A was considered the best interviewer by her colleagues, and was most popular with them. The interviewers in *both* sections disliked working in a competitive atmosphere, but the difference in values made it possible to curb competitive practices in only one of the groups.

The group more concerned with productivity was less productive. As indicated in Table 1, 59 per cent of all job openings received in Section A were filled, in contrast to 67 per cent of those in Section B. Although the more competitive interviewers in Section A made more placements, the group as a whole made fewer placements. Why were competitiveness and productivity directly related for individuals but inversely for groups? In their eagerness to make many placements the interviewers in Section A often ignored the effect of their actions on their relations with colleagues. The prevalence of such competitive behavior weakened social cohesion, and this in turn reduced operating efficiency.

The productive interviewer in Section A tried to hoard jobs and also to prevent others from doing so by asking them for the job orders they had received over the telephone. Both these practices alienated his coworkers, whose co-operation he needed if he were to perform well. Often an interviewer paid another a compliment about his work or her apparel, or told a joke, in order to restore more cordial relations. The most competitive interviewer was in the habit of taking time out to "fool around" with her coworkers and was proud that "nevertheless" she made more placements than anybody else. Actually this compensating friendliness, which made her popular despite her competitiveness, helped her to be so productive. Only those members of Section A who made special efforts to mend their interpersonal relations were able to make many placements, but this compensatory behavior was not necessary in the more cohesive Section B.

The status anxiety generated by the evaluation on the basis of his performance records is most acute for the individual who does not feel integrated in his work group and therefore seeks to derive social recognition through excellence in his task and through the consequent approval of superiors. Friendly relations with coworkers made the standing of the individual in the cohesive group independent of his productivity, especially since fast work was disapproved of as a sign of superficial service. Of course social cohesion is no guarantee against anxiety in a bureaucratic situation. But when threats to civil-service status did not exist, social cohesion reduced anxiety over productivity by divesting it of its significance as the status symbol in the work group. The hypothesis that the cohesion of the group and the competitive behavior of the individual in the non-cohesive group had the same effect of lessening status anxiety explains the paradox that the *less competitive group* and the *more competitive individual* in the competitive group were particularly productive.

Sine Ira et Studio

Ideally, as Weber says, bureaucratic officials meet the public in "a spirit of formalistic impersonality, '*sine ira et studio*,' without hatred or passion, and hence without affection or enthusiasm." This requirement assures equitable treatment of clients and rational rather than emotionally dominated operations. But if this is the ideal, it is not necessarily realized in practice.

The staff of Department X spent most of their working time talking to clients, and these interactions constituted their major source of work satisfaction. When asked, "When do you get a special kick out of your job?" interviewers uniformly answered with instances involving assistance to their clientele, either workers or employers. Most of them spontaneously referred to expressions of gratitude to exemplify special satisfaction in their work. A few kept a file of letters of thanks in their desks. Some mentioned that they would enjoy their work more if they had the opportunity of talking to all clients after they had been placed.

The exercise of discretionary power in dealing with clients appears to be a condition for work satisfaction of this kind. If the interviewer merely followed regulations, he found that "the work gets very boring; you ask the qualifications of an applicant, and send him out." But "when you do something more than is called for, you enjoy it." An interviewer was free to offer some extra help to clients whose qualifications, in his judgment, warranted it; and this power of decision enhanced his work satisfaction and supplied incentives for exerting greater effort.

Helping clients was a gratifying experience for interviewers, regardless of their attitudes toward these poor, unskilled workers. Interviewers who identified with this group welcomed the opportunity to assist them, while those who felt condescension toward them obtained satisfaction from their relative superiority of status. The interviewer's attitude, however, did influence the type of client he was most eager to assist. Most of these white-collar employees favored applicants with middle-class characteristics, whose values were similar to their own; they made special efforts for clients who, in the words of one of them, "are very personable and very anxious to work." A minority of the interviewers, on the other hand, said that they gave special attention to applicants whose need for jobs was most urgent.

The satisfaction that interviewers derived from helping clients motivated them to exert greater effort in their work, but it also endangered their impartiality, since they were more interested in serving some clients than others. In short, bureaucratically irrelevant criteria tended to affect operations. To restore uniformity and impartiality, superiors attempted to channel work satisfaction toward impersonal sources. They stressed that their subordinates should remain detached in their contacts with clients, finding rewards in assisting unemployed workers in general rather than in helping individuals.

The interviewers' bureaucratic impartiality was also disturbed by differences with the agency's clients. Arguments were relatively frequent, particularly in production-minded Section A. These conflicts were disturbing, for the antagonism they generated was followed by a feeling of guilt in these service-oriented employees. Informal discussion among interviewers developed as a social mechanism to ease the tension that sharp differences with clients had produced.

Most private discussions in the office dealt with clients. "Either it's a funny incident, something an applicant said or did that's supposed to be hilarious, or it's the type, 'Look what this applicant did to me!' " Complaining about clients or ridiculing them sometimes released the interviewer's aggressive feelings in a harmless fashion, but not every complaint can be explained as a discharge of aggression. The interviewers who administered most sanctions against clients initiated a disproportionately large number of private conversations with their colleagues, not so much in order to vent hostility against clients as to calm the interviewer's doubts about the fairness of his treatment of them. In these discussions the sympathetic listener identified with the speaker; by his gestures and comments, his amusement at the stupidity of the client, his amazement at the client's impertinence, he condemned the client's behavior and bestowed social approval upon the decision the speaker had made. As a fellow-believer in the service ideals of the agency, moreover, the listener was qualified to justify the speaker's action in terms of these values. The assent implicit in appreciative listening therefore dispelled the mental discomfort of an employee whose action had violated his ideals.

The interviewer's jokes, just like his complaints, served to absolve him from guilt feelings. Complaints were nearly always made to a single colleague, but jokes were often told to a group. Since the humor of jokes provided a motive for listening to them, they lent themselves to being told to an audience and to being repeated by other persons; and in the process of being repeated they lost their uniqueness. Since jokes tended to deal with generic client types, most members of the audience could remember some of their own clients who "do things like that." Complaints, which were listened to as an expression of solidarity with the speaker, *presupposed* social cohesion, whereas jokes helped *create* it by uniting a group in the pleasant experience of laughing together.

Telling jokes reduced the tendency of conflicts to disrupt operations, but it did so at a social cost. The integrative experience of common amusement was based on common disidentification with the ridiculous clients. Stupid, hostile, impertinent, or mentally deranged applicants, although admittedly exceptional, were often responsible for conflicts and lent themselves particularly well to being ridiculed. Thus funny stories concentrated on these clients, producing a stereotype with which the interviewer could hardly sympathize. Moreover, the social approval indicated by laughing at the inconsiderate treatment of these clients tended to create group norms. Jokes not only dissolved uncertainty and self-reproach but also inhibited such feelings from arising in similar cases in the future. They helped transform the inconsiderate treatment of clients from a private exception into a socially approved practice.

Since relations to clients were not emotionally neutral, the question arises whether Negro and white applicants were given the same service. The operations of this agency were especially well protected against the intrusion of the prevailing racial prejudices. According to official rules, occupational qualifications alone were relevant in deciding on an applicant's case, and these rules were constantly reinforced by superiors' admonitions to conduct interviews on an impersonal plane. Moreover, an anti-discrimination law in the state prohibited interviewers, not only from engaging in ethnic discrimination themselves, but also from accepting an employer's request that specified the skin color, religion, or nationality of the worker. Finally, the members of this department (eleven out of the twenty-four were themselves members of minority ethnic groups) personally shared the value commitments of this law and presumably would not have discriminated against Negro clients even if this had not been forbidden. Prejudice, however, is subtle, and an individual is often unaware of a bias betrayed only by his actual behavior. Manifestly, rules prohibiting discrimination cannot prevent the influence of bias lying below the threshold of personal awareness.

Was discrimination to be observed among the interviewers? Only three of the fifteen interviewers were Negroes, while 55 per cent of the applicants interviewed in Department X were Negroes. Had there been bias in treatment, it would presumably have found expression in a disproportionately large number of white referrals. But in one section the proportion of white referrals to all referrals was equal to the proportion of white clients to all clients, and in the other two sections it was considerably *smaller*. Interviewers appear to have *favored* Negroes in their selections.

The absence of discrimination among interviewers, or the reversal of the usual anti-Negro discrimination, could have been caused by the attitudes of these particular persons, but during the three months he spent in daily contact with them and watched the interactions of this ethnically mixed group, the author did not find any indication of biased attitudes. The hypothesis is advanced that it was rather structural differences in the work situation that were responsible for these findings. As one interviewer explained, "We get only very low-paying jobs, and Negroes are willing to accept less, because they're forced to do so." The greater alacrity with which Negroes accepted the poorly paid jobs available made them preferable clients and more than neutralized any bias against them that might otherwise have existed.

The greater their concern with making a good showing on production records, the more effectively interviewers excluded all considerations from their official decisions except those that helped maximize placements. Thus the production-conscious members of Section A used a disproportionately large number of their job openings for Negroes, who were easier to place. In contrast, the less production-oriented interviewers in Section B referred Negroes and whites in equal proportions, despite the Negroes' greater eagerness to take jobs.

Moreover, the more concerned an *individual* was with productivity, the more favorably did he treat Negroes. The three Negro interviewers, whose ethnic identification and bureaucratic interest reinforced each other, referred larger proportions of Negro clients than most white interviewers did. The interviewer whose proportion of Negro referrals was highest, however, was not a Negro, but she was the most competitive person in the department.

Thus, whether individuals or groups are compared, the white interviewers who were most anxious to make many placements were least likely to allow personal prejudice to influence their treatment of clients. These findings have some implications for social action intended to change discriminatory practices. It is often held that it is impossible to abolish discrimination in a specific institutional setting until the prejudiced attitudes that prevail in our culture have disappeared. These data suggest that if objectives of overriding importance can be made to govern organized activities, discrimination will be eliminated regardless of the presence of prejudice.

The Dynamics of Bureaucratic Structure

Weber conceived of bureacracy as the optimum social mechanism for ensuring efficiency in administration and also as a form of social organization with specific characteristics. Both of these criteria, however, cannot properly be part of the definition: the relation between the attributes and consequences of a social institution is a question for empirical verification. Weber's discussion can be interpreted in one of two ways. Either he intended to define bureacracy by specifying its formal characteristics and hypothesized its superior operating efficiency, or he intended to define it as that administrative apparatus that maximizes efficiency, and advanced hypotheses about organizational attributes that would typically have this effect.

In terms of the second alternative bureaucracies can be regarded as institutionalized modes of organizing social conduct in order (1) to transform exceptional problems into the routine duties of experts, and (2) to effect the co-ordination of specialized tasks. The social arrangements most suitable for these purposes are not the same in different cultures. Thus in the Germany of Weber's day, where social relations in the family and in society generally tended to be authoritarian, and where lack of education limited the qualifications of subordinate officials, strict hierarchical control may have been the most efficient method of bureaucratic operation. However, where equality in social relations is highly valued and where a much higher level of popular education has been reached, as in the United States today, to grant subordinates considerable discretionary power may be a more efficient system of administration. Similarly, in a culture oriented toward tradition, bureaucratic efficiency would probably require less change in organization than in a younger culture, where progress is a central value.

In the organization studied, efficient operations depended on a readiness to reorganize. Often social patterns that served important operational functions also produced conditions that impeded the effective attainment of organizational objectives. And these emergent needs sometimes gave rise to new practices to meet them. The introduction of statistical records, for instance, both improved placement operations and engendered competitiveness, which interfered with the agency's service. In response to these new organizational needs social innovations developed that restored operating efficiency. Interviewers in one section devised methods for discouraging competitive tendencies, and this group became more productive than the one that continued competitive practices.

Spontaneous adjustments that solved incipient operational problems often developed among the office staff in the course of their work. What were the bureaucratic conditions that accounted for this pattern of self-adjustment, which was essential for efficiency? The various cases of persistent dysfunctions suggest five prerequisites of adjustive development: (1) at least some security in employment; (2) the absence of basic conflict between work group and top management; (3) a professional orientation toward the performance of duties; (4) established work groups that command the allegiance of their members; (5) organizational needs that are experienced as disturbing.

1. Persons can originate new procedures only if they have relative job security; where one's job hangs in the balance ritualistic adherence to the existing order is the norm. Interviewers in Section A, while on probation for their civil-service appointment, were too anxious to comply with the demands of superiors to

be able to discourage competitive practices. The members of Section B, who already held permanent civil-service positions and thus felt free to co-operate in disregarding the official statistical records, were able thereby to improve productivity.

2. Employment security engenders the psychological freedom of action that enables individuals to initiate adjustments, but it does not guarantee that these will further the objectives of the agency. In private industry, for example, restriction of output among factory workers is a common adjustment designed to protect the economic interest of workers against management. Most unofficial practices observed in the agency, however—including some that violated official rules—contributed to operating efficiency, in part because the civil-service system eliminates one basic source of conflict between management and subordinates. Private management controls both employment conditions and operations, while in government agencies management controls operations but not salaries and personnel procedures, which are determined by the Civil Service Commission. Since the rating given him influences his chances of advancement, his economic interest may bring an *individual* into conflict with superiors. However, the *collective* economic interest of agency employees in the state budget affects their relations with the agency administrators only in the sense of bringing them closer, for all are interested in legislation that benefits civil servants.

3. If tenure is not to result in private adaptations detrimental to the interests of the organization, a professional orientation must prevail—a general identi-

fication with norms that make the attainment of professional objectives a source of satisfaction. Civil-service personnel are more likely to have such a professional orientation toward their work, for only applicants with the technical training required for a job are appointed, and the relative security of civil-service positions encourages loyalty to the organization and its values. A professional orientation is also fostered by a system of evaluation based on results achieved rather than techniques used. If the interviewers criticized statistical records as unprofessional, it was in part because they felt that the particular indexes measured only superficial accomplishments.

4. A professional orientation also engenders anxiety: the greater their interest in professional objectives and the fewer the external restraints on their method of achieving them, the more likely it is that civil servants will feel anxious. This feeling can be relieved by co-operative and congenial interaction with coworkers, which gives all of them a feeling of security in the work situation. The social support of the group also makes it easier to adopt new practices, since it lessens the need to find emotional security in familiar routines. Social cohesion, therefore, paves the way for the development of new adjustments. When competitive practices interfered with the work of interviewers, individual efforts to check them were ineffective, while the collective enforcement of co-operation in an entire group was effective. Unofficial practices that met organizational needs were most prevalent in cohesive groups, because they alone could effectively enforce informal norms: their members value their interper-

sonal relations, and this makes them subject to the control of the group.

5. No unofficial adjustment will occur, even under otherwise favorable conditions, unless the persons involved feel that an organizational need is disturbing. For example, more clients than could be served came to the employment agency because when receptionists sent them home, the latter set the clients' reappointment dates earlier than they should have. Since this did not interfere directly with departmental operations, no one—neither clerks nor interviewers nor even supervisors—was interested in finding ways to limit the flow of clients. In such cases adjustment must depend on the hierarchical distribution of responsibility and authority, for the wider responsibility of superior officials includes coping with indirect impediments to operations. Ideally the superiors should not ordinarily complete the necessary changes directly, but only begin them by creating conditions that will make subordinates experience the organizational needs as disturbing. Thus the necessary innovations will in general evolve spontaneously, and supervisors will have to intercede by officially instituting new procedures only occasionally, as a last resort.

Bureaucracies in a democratic society pose a paradox. In a mass society democracy depends on bureaucratic institutions, but the concentration of power in the hands of a few men in business and government threatens democratic institutions. If this is a paradox, it is also a challenge. Our democratic institutions, which originated at a time when bureaucracies were in a rudimentary stage, are not designed to cope with their control. We cannot turn the clock back and return to the New England township, where unbureaucratic democracy was possible; and we would not if we could, since we value the products that modern bureaucracies supply. To extend our institutions by developing democratic methods for governing bureaucracies is, perhaps, the crucial problem of our age. In this study of a bureaucracy's internal structure it has not been possible to do more than raise this problem and suggest some general requirements of bureaucratic efficiency.

A fundamental revision of the conception of rationality in administration can be expected, for the present assumption that the rational pursuit of bureaucratic objectives requires that most members of the organization virtually abstain from exercising rational judgment ignores the dynamic complexity of a bureaucracy. Many jobs cannot be circumscribed by specific rules that obviate the need for exercising judgment, and attempts to do so impede effective performance. Moreover, efficiency depends on recurrent modifications of operating methods and is thus lessened during the time lag between the appearance of operational difficulties and the official establishment of remedies. In contrast, if standardization is achieved by specifying results rather than techniques, necessary adjustments will tend to emerge spontaneously in work groups.

Suggestions for Further Reading

ROBERT K. MERTON *et al.* (eds.). *Reader in Bureaucracy* (Glencoe, Illinois: Free Press, 1952). A wide collection of readings, including excerpts from most of the following works. See in particular Carl J. Friedrich's criticism of Weber's ideal-typical analysis of bureaucracy (pp. 27–32).

MAX WEBER. *Essays in Sociology* (New York: Oxford University Press, 1946); *The Theory of Social and Economic Organization* (New York: Oxford University Press, 1947). The classic theory of bureaucracy, presented as one example of the "rationalization" of the modern world.

CHESTER I. BARNARD. *The Functions of the Executive* (Cambridge: Harvard University Press, 1938). An attempt to correct with appropriate theory and exemplifications the "four principal errors" of bureaucrats—"an oversimplification of the economy of organization life; a disregard of the fact and of the necessity of informal organization; an inversion of emphasis upon the objective and the subjective aspects of authority; and a confusion of morality with responsibility."

HERBERT A. SIMON. *Administrative Behavior: A Study of Decision-Making Processes in Administrative Organization* (New York: Macmillan, 1947). A study of formal organization and administration, with a stress on how policy decisions are made.

ROBERT K. MERTON. *Social Theory and Social Structure* (Glencoe, Illinois: Free Press, 1949). A collection of essays by one of America's foremost sociologists, including several that develop functional analysis as used in this study by Peter Blau.

About the Authors

BERNARD BERELSON, now director of the Behavioral Sciences Program of the Ford Foundation, has been professor of social sciences and dean of the Graduate Library School at the University of Chicago. During World War II he served with the Foreign Broadcast Intelligence Service of the Federal Communications Commission. He received his Ph.D. from the University of Chicago and is the author of a number of books and articles on public opinion and communications, including another work on voting behavior.

PETER M. BLAU teaches sociology at the University of Chicago. He has also taught at Cornell University and Wayne University. He received his Ph.D. from Columbia University. He is the author of several articles and has written another book on the theory of bureaucracy.

JAMES S. COLEMAN is a research associate at the Bureau of Applied Social Research of Columbia University. During 1955–56 he was a fellow at the Center for Advanced Study in the Behavioral Sciences at Stanford.

MARY EVANS COLLINS teaches psychology at Sarah Lawrence College and is studying the social factors related to adjustment in college. She received her

M.A. from the University of Wisconsin, and has been associated with the Commission on Community Interrelations of the American Jewish Congress and with the market-research division of the Psychological Corporation in New York.

MORTON DEUTSCH, a professor of psychology at New York University, is doing research on trust in interpersonal relations. He received his Ph.D. from the Massachusetts Institute of Technology. His publications include reports on a number of theoretical and experimental studies on small groups.

HAZEL GAUDET (Mrs. Graham Erskine), presently engaged in free-lance research in Nevada, has conducted studies for various universities and civic organizations. After receiving her M.A. from George Washington University she worked on surveys with the Office of War Information in New York and London and with the Columbia Broadcasting System. Her publications include a number of studies in communications and labor research.

PAUL F. LAZARSFELD is a professor of sociology at Columbia University, a past president of the American Association for Public Opinion Research, an elected member of the Academy of Arts and Sciences. He received his Ph.D. from the University of Vienna. His many publications include significant contributions in public opinion research, voting behavior, and methodology.

SEYMOUR MARTIN LIPSET is professor of sociology at the University of California, Berkeley. He received his Ph.D. from Columbia University, and taught there and at the University of Toronto. He is the author of

262

Agrarian Socialism, and (with Reinhard Bendix) editor of *Class, Status and Power.*

LEO LOWENTHAL has been chief of the New York staff of the Office of Research and Intelligence, U. S. Information Agency; director of the evaluation staff, International Broadcasting Service, U. S. Department of State; and New York editor for the Institute of Social Research. He received his Ph.D. in political science from the University of Frankfurt, and he is the author of a number of works on popular culture, the sociology of literature, psychological warfare, and international communications research.

MARTIN A. TROW is on the faculty of Bennington College, and was formerly a research associate at the Bureau of Applied Social Research of Columbia University.

WILLIAM PETERSEN received his Ph.D. in sociology from Columbia University. He has taught at Columbia University, Smith College, and the University of California, Berkeley, and he is now on the faculty of the University of Colorado. He has published articles in various magazines, and is the author of Planned Migration.

ANCHOR BOOKS